MW01259484

 **A gift for you**

For the Depeche Mode fan who has everything.... Could be fun reading about how DM changed someone else's life and inspired them in their healing? Let me know how it is! 😳 with love, V
From Vineet Chander

...ode

Saved by Depeche Mode

An Epic Journey of Healing and Remission Through Music

Jasmine Singh

Published by Game Changer Publishing
Back cover image: Maria Turner, Black Diamond Boudoir

Paperback ISBN: 978-1-964811-68-0
Hardcover ISBN: 978-1-964811-70-3
Digital ISBN: 978-1-964811-71-0

Disclaimer: This manuscript references the band name Depeche Mode and may allude to lyrics from their songs for illustrative purposes. The author acknowledges that Depeche Mode and their associated trademarks, music, and lyrics are the exclusive property of their respective owners. The use of these elements in this work is solely for the purpose of commentary, criticism, analysis, and educational reference, and is not intended to infringe upon the rights of the copyright holders.

www.GameChangerPublishing.com

Dedication

This book is dedicated to my miracle baby and my heart.
I love you so much!

Acknowledgments

A very heartfelt thank you to everyone who was a part of my journey.
I am so incredibly GRATEFUL to you!

My spiritual team

My beautiful daughter

My mom, dad, massive, masserji, sister, brother, and immediate family

Game Changer Publishing and staff

My cousins and extended family

My friends, my soul tribe (you know who you are)

My podcast partner, Alexander

My Art Institute family all over North America

My SoléAna Stables family - please visit www.https://soleanastables.org/ to learn more

My health family - 24 Hour Fitness Aqua Zumba class, Club Pilates, Massage Heights & Tuscan Villa Nails & Spa.

My spiritual advisors - Toni Bubb - http://www.tonibubb.com & Mystic Molly - https://www.mysticmolly1111.com/

My amazing doctors, specialists, pharmacists, all of their staff:

    Ms. Brenda Henning - Psychologist

    Mrs. Dolly Patel - Pharmacist - Royal Pharmacy

    Dr. Alexander Butkevich - Cardiologist

    Dr. Amina Malik - Surgical Ophthalmologist

    Dr. Angie Staller - Urologist

    Dr. Bincy Abraham - Gastroenterologist (Colon, UC)

Ms. Brenda Henning - Therapist

Dr. Charles Popemey - Neurologist

Dr. Christine Swade - Family Practice

Dr. Chukwuma Egwim - Gastroenterologist (liver)

Dr. David Bloome - Orthopedic Surgeon (feet)

Dr. Dean Smith - Orthopedic Surgeon (hands, wrists, elbows)

Dr. Eddie Huang - Orthopedic Surgeon (hips)

Dr. Eric Powitsky - ENT

Dr. J Edward Hernandez - Rheumatologist

Dr. Jacqueline Rice-McKenzie - ER Physician Specialist and Medical Cannabis Consultant

Dr. James Wallace - General Surgeon

Dr. John Butler - Infectious Diseases

Dr. Joseph Toothaker-Alvarez - Pain Management

Dr. Kenneth Matthis - Orthopedic Surgeon (knees)

Ms. Kristina Gomez - Psychologist

Dr. Manpreet Mangat - Pulmonologist

Dr. Mary Moore - Dermatologist

Dr. Robert Fullick - Orthopedic Surgeon (shoulders)

Dr. Rosa Guerra - Gynecologic Oncologist

Dr. Selma Raheem - Psychiatrist

Dr. Shahid Ali - Gastroenterologist (Colon, UC)

Dr. Sonia Eapen - Endocrinologist

Dr. Willam McGarvey - Orthopedic Surgeon (feet, ankles)

Eye Center of Texas - Dr. Julie Ngo - Ophthalmologist

Texas Original - Medical Cannabis Dispensary/Houston

Texas Goodblend - Medical Cannabis Dispensary/Houston

Memorial Hermann Sports Medicine & Rehabilitation - PT Nandita Mahendra

Vision Source - Dr. Dipak Kalani - Optometrist

Dr. Martha Aguilar - Rheumatologist (retired)

And, drumroll please…

Dr. Thaddues Hume - my OG Orthopedic Surgeon (retired),
whom I pressured to replace my knees in 1994
I'm so grateful to you for listening to me, and I hope you are enjoying retirement!

Read This First

Just to say thanks for buying and reading my book,
I would like to share a playlist of all the songs included within
the book that have been a part of my journey to who I am today.
Thank you!

Scan the QR Code Here:

Saved by Depeche Mode

*An Epic Journey of Healing and
Remission Through Music*

Jasmine Singh

www.GameChangerPublishing.com

Table of Contents

INTRODUCTION

Y ou're probably wondering why the hell I named my memoir *Saved by Depeche Mode*. It's because they did. Their music saved my soul. I'll tell you how in the next few hours or however long it takes for you to read this book.

And who the heck am I, anyway? When people ask me who I am, what makes me tick, or what my story is, it's so challenging for me to keep it to a 30-second elevator pitch. Initially, it started at 30 seconds, but over 40 very long years, it evolved into me asking, "Do you want to know my story in a nutshell?" or "How much time do you have?" because it's a lot.

Since you bought my book and are currently reading it, I'm assuming you are in it for the long haul. So, please enjoy the ride. This is a crazy story.

In a nutshell, I've been struggling with autoimmune diseases for over 40 years. I've spent four years in a wheelchair and have had 36 surgeries, mainly joint replacements and fusions. I've had my knee replaced TWICE in my lifetime, and I'm 53. Yeah, I know. It's a lot. I've been married, had a miracle baby, gotten divorced, and thought my life was over. More importantly, I was *ready* for my life to be over.

This is 53-year-old Jasmine telling my poor, terrified inner child who's cowering in the corner that everything is going to be okay. I got you! We are going to be okay. I promise! I've done a lot of internal work to get to this point. I will share stories about the things that I've done, what's helped, and what hasn't. Basically, I'm just a regular human who happens to have been dealt a pretty shitty hand in the health department and been through a lot. I've had so many surgeries and procedures and been put under so many times that it's shocking I'm not brain-dead from all of the anesthesia I've had! Lol. And after all of the pain medications and opioids I've taken over the last 40 years, it's a blessing I never got addicted and withered my life away!

So, why now? It's been 40 years. Why did I wait until now to share my story? Because I finally have the "ending" that I've been waiting four decades for.

In August of 2023, I found out that the *one* autoimmune disease, rheumatoid arthritis (RA), the *bane* of my existence and the very first one that I was diagnosed with at the age of 13, is *finally* in remission.

That's why.

For the first time in 40 years.

That was such a huge moment in my life, and it hit me that I finally had the ending to my book! I've been wanting to write a book for the last 20-plus years, but for some reason or other, it just never came to fruition. One of the biggest reasons is that I can't physically *write* a book. My hands have always been in pretty bad shape due to the joint damage from RA.

If only one person reads this book and gets some value from it, my job is done. I consider it a success if even just a single reader thinks, *Wow, she was able to accomplish so much after all the shit that she's been through, so why the hell can't I do it, too?*

That's why I feel like it's important for me to share. I'm not special, I'm not a superhero, and this wasn't magic. And I don't want to gate-keep anything that has helped me get to where I am today. And let me tell you, I have tried everything you can imagine, from Western medicine to Eastern medicine. I even lived in India for six months while confined to a wheelchair!

The purpose of this book is to give hope to my readers so that they, too, can overcome the struggles they are going through. It IS possible to overcome anything! I'm living proof! If you believe and have faith, you will ALWAYS be guided on the right path. There will ALWAYS be light in the darkness. Always. And you don't have to be religious to believe this. As above, so below. We all have the power to heal ourselves. We simply need to activate it and tap into it.

So many people are struggling with autoimmune diseases or going through something else in their lives, whether it be financial, mental, physical, or marital. Many want to give up, thinking, *I just don't want to do this anymore. I don't want to be here. I want to stop. I don't have any hope. I don't have any reason to go on.* Trust me, I have been there. THAT WAS ME! It is a horrible, horrible place to be. And trying to find that *one* positive, that *one* piece of hope, that *one* thing that really makes all the difference in the world and brings you peace and happiness, is easier said than done. In fact, it's fucking hard to do. But I found it. That's what music did for me. Music is my positive; music is my hope.

I tried to take all of this negative shit that I was dealing with, all of these horrible things that were happening to me, and do my best to find peace in my creativity, holding on for dear life. Dancing, music, meditation, drawing, painting, creating, self-care – they are my zen.

When good things and moments come to an end in your life, it's not over. It simply means that you are shifting, that you are evolving. There are other things for you to do and look forward to. And you're not alone. Loneliness is such a HEAVY emotion. You can be surrounded by people who love you and still be incredibly lonely. I know I was. I knew that I would get very emotional writing this book. I knew that I would get very emotional telling and sharing my story because I lived it. It happened to me. All of this shit happened to ME!

It's amazing to me that I was able to escape the darkness and emerge on the other side *looking* the way that I do, *feeling* the way that I do. And I would be lying to you if I told you it was easy. That's the *furthest* thing from the truth. It was hard as hell to get here. But if I can do it, then anybody can. That's my hope: That someone will read this, hear my journey, hear everything that I went through, and find inspiration – and laugh with me because it is funny, too. There are some genuinely funny parts, and I'm a goofball. I try to find the humor in every single situation, regardless of how dire it is! You'll see when you read those stories.

I've always shared my story with others in a positive way because I don't want anyone to feel sorry for me or think, *Dang, she's lived a depressing life. Sucks to be her.* Because I didn't, I simply did what I needed to do to survive. So, I want you to laugh with me because I found the humor in all of these stories. Everything that's happened to me is hilarious, daunting, and overwhelming, and I'm now ready to share it all with you.

I am so grateful for this opportunity! Please take my hand, and I will guide you along my journey. Rest assured, it's all going to be okay in the end. That's why I wanted to start it off by talking about my remission; I want to tell you the ending first. The remission is good. I'm good. I made it through. I'm alive. I'm still here. And THIS is my life's purpose: to share my story. So, sit back, relax, and let me show you the "World in My Eyes."

CHAPTER 1

PRECIOUS ROSY

PRECIOUS

Depeche Mode

"Precious" is about an innocent soul that should not have to suffer.
Does God indeed have a master plan for us?
That only HE understands?
If so, I hope He sees through your eyes, my reader...

I was born on November 16, 1970, in Ajmer, Rajasthan, India. I grew up in a very conservative Sikh family and lived in India for just a year and a half before coming to the U.S. When I was born, I was incredibly light-skinned, which is not very typical for an Indian person. My sweet massi (my mom's sister) took one look at me and said, "Oh, my gosh. She has the rosiest cheeks." In Punjabi, she said, "Yeh toh hamara rose hah." Translation: "She is our Rose."

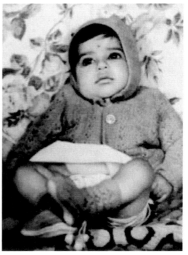

This is the only baby photo of me - circa 1971

That's how I got the nickname Rosy growing up. My nanaji (my mom's dad) named me Jasminder because the hospital insisted on having a name for the birth certificate. Traditionally, Sikhs are supposed to consult our Holy Book, Guru Granth Sahib, for the first letter of a baby's name, but we didn't have a chance. The hospital insisted on a name right away, so he chose Jasminder.

When I arrived in the U.S. a year and a half later, my dad was already there. In 1970, right before I was born, he'd moved to Queens in New York City. I would find out later in life that he and his best friend rang in the new year in Times Square in 1971! I moved to the States with my mom and sister, who is three years older than me. According to my mom, I was a rambunctious, overactive, extroverted kid. I smiled all the time at everyone. Basically, I was a super-social child filled with energy. My sister was the complete opposite: very introverted, quiet, and academic. That'll come into play later on in my story.

According to my mother, as soon as I got off that plane in New York, I bolted into the airport. My sister had to rein me in, and she kept telling my mom, "Man, I can't do this anymore. She doesn't listen to me and just keeps running around the airport."

I don't remember a whole lot from our time in New York because I was just a year and a half old, but my mom has shared a lot of fun stories with me. One time, I was jumping on the bed and fell face-first into the nightstand. My forehead hit the corner, and my mom, fresh from India, had no idea what to do. She went to an Indian neighbor who lived a few doors down (we were in an apartment complex), and the woman told my mom to burn a cotton ball, put the ashes in the wound, and cover it with a Band-Aid®. Who knew? Lol. So, I had ashes on my forehead, and I still have that scar, my very first.

I have memories of visiting the Statue of Liberty. We used to go all the time and take along our friends and family who came to visit from India or other places in the States. We also went to the World Trade Center. I was terrified of both because they were so big! And those Statue of Liberty stairs –

have you ever gone up and down them? Back then, you used to be able to go inside the statue, and there were spiral stairs. You either went up or down; there was no other option. You couldn't get off, and you couldn't stop. You just kept going. It seemed like a never-ending staircase.

Once, I cried the entire way up and wailed the entire way down because I was terrified of those stupid stairs. Typically, I was very adventurous, the type of kid who was always doing things that I wasn't supposed to be doing. I was definitely braver than my sister. But I think I was too young for those stairs. I probably shouldn't have gone up them, but I did.

From New York, we went to New Jersey. My dad had gotten a job in Philadelphia, so he commuted back and forth. We lived in Cherry Hill and had this badass 1969 baby blue Chevy Impala that my dad bought, which, nowadays, is such an amazing ride! We didn't think that much of the car back then, except that it was a CAR! And not a lot of people had cars. We certainly didn't need a car in NY because of the awesome transit system and trains.

We lived in a great apartment in Cherry Hill. One time, my sister came in crying. I asked her, "What is wrong with you? What happened?" It turned out that her friend had hit her, and they'd gotten into some sort of scuffle. My mom loves telling me this story, by the way, and sharing it with anybody I bring over to the house. Without hesitation, I took my sister's hand and marched her down the stairs. "Who hit you?" I asked. When she pointed the culprit out, I punched the girl and told her, "Don't you EVER touch my sister again!" Then I went back into the house like a BOSS. My sister was mean to me and never really wanted to play with me, but it didn't matter. I loved her! She was my sister, and NOBODY was allowed to fuck with her. That's the type of person that I've always been. Don't mess with my loved ones because I will take you out.

I always got in trouble. My sister had this badass record player that she absolutely cherished. And music was my thing, man. I loved listening to music. This was the 70s. It's not like we had streaming services and all this other shit that we have nowadays. We were limited to a regular old radio and a TV that only picked up two channels – and a black-and-white TV at that.

One day, my friend came over, and my mom realized that she didn't hear us playing. Naturally, she KNEW I was up to something because it was quiet – TOO quiet. My friend and I had snuck into my sister's closet and found the record player.

When my mom came into the room, she found us in the closet, and there was a broken record on the floor. I had broken one of my sister's records. My mom was livid. "Oh, my God," she said. "Your sister's going to kill you."

"I just wanted to hear the music and stuff, and it broke," I replied.

"How'd you break the record?" she asked.

Without hesitation, I picked up another record, put it on the record player, and stepped on it.

My mom laughed so hard that she couldn't even get mad at me. "I can't believe you just did that," she said. "I thought you said you were playing the record?"

"I was!" I said, and now I'd broken a second record just showing her how I'd done it the first time around. I'm fairly certain that I was jealous that my sister had a record player and I didn't. So, that's just how I've always been: getting into innocent trouble for having too much energy.

I often came home from school with candy, and my mom would ask me, "Where are you getting all this candy from?"

"Well," I said, "my teacher gave it to me."

"Why did she give it to you?"

"So I would be quiet and stay in my seat."

So, I was getting BRIBES from my teacher: "If you stay quiet and stay in your seat and quit being so rambunctious, I will give you candy." And she did. I freaking loved being social! I loved growing up like this, but I was also struggling with my identity, asking myself, *Am I American because I live here now, or am I Indian?* My family was very traditional, and Americans were VERY different than Indians in every way.

I always wanted to wear my hair down like all of the other little girls. You didn't see a whole lot of diversity back then. Most folks around us were white. That lack of diversity caused some issues. Because we were Sikh, we didn't celebrate Christmas or other traditional holidays. Hell, I actually got kicked out of Catholic school for telling all of the kids that there was no such thing as Santa Claus. To be fair, that was what I had been

Apparently I used to love hanging out under the sink with the trash can and sodas - lol!

taught. To this day, that still kind of shocks me. It's kind of extreme to get expelled simply for telling kids that there's no such thing as Santa Claus. Oh, well!

We were in New Jersey for about a year, and then my dad got a job in Houston, Texas. So, we made the trek to Houston in 1976, and I have been here ever since. Soon after moving, my mom came to pick me up from kindergarten one day, but I never walked out. She knew that something had happened, that I had been kept back, and she was like, "What's going on?" Finally, she put the car in park, walked into the school, and said, "Where's my kid?" Then sees me on my hands and knees, scrubbing the floor with tears streaming down my face, and she's like, "What the heck? What did my kid do?" she asked.

"She was supposed to be coloring on her paper," the teacher replied, "but instead, she colored on the floor." So, I got into trouble. I had to stay after school, but you know, teachers didn't usually tell your parents ahead of time back then. We didn't have cell phones, teachers didn't have phones in their classrooms, and there was no email. So, she had to walk into the school and find me scrubbing the floor with tears streaming down my face. Poor Rosy. I really loved to draw, though! That became one of my jams! Art was my thing. Drawing was my thing. That was always what I wanted to do.

At first, we lived in an apartment. My mom was pregnant, and we didn't know the sex of the baby until the birth. When my brother was born, I wasn't very happy because I wanted a little sister. My older sister got to boss me around all the time, so I wanted a little sister that I could boss around, too. He would squirm in my arms when I would hold him sometimes, so I would just let go and drop him on the floor, which I know is terrible to this day. It's absolutely terrible. I love my brother so much. I absolutely adore my brother. My brother is six years younger than me, and he and I are still close, closer than my sister and me. He and I bonded through so much of my trauma, especially later in my story.

After my brother was born, we moved into our first house on Apothecary Lane. I still remember the street! I loved playing outside and was very athletic. I loved riding my bike, playing kickball, and running. My dad got bikes for my sister and me when we were living in that house, and we would ride up and down our street. She didn't like to play outside as much as I did. I was always outside. I was one of those stereotypical Gen Xers who would go outside in the morning, get on my bike, play with my friends, pretend I was a bus driver on my bike, and stop at every mailbox. We all did this, right? You would stop, open the door to your bus, let all the kids in, and drop them off on the next driveway – some imaginary fun! My friends and I would play kickball, basketball, and gymnastics in the yard, and we would just be crazy! We'd also walk around the neighborhood, knock on other friends' doors, and say, "Hey, can you come out and play? Let's stay out," and we would stay out all day long.

I would fall off my bike sometimes because I was going too fast or trying to pop a wheelie, or I would get my foot stuck in the pedals or the chain, and the chain would come off my bike and just rip up my leg. I would run into the house, terrified that my mom was going to see it and make me stay indoors. After cleaning myself up in the bathroom, I'd throw on some triple antibiotic cream and a shit-ton of Band-Aids and go right back out again. It wouldn't be until later that night that my mom would see the Band-Aids on my legs and be like, "What the hell happened to you?" This was the total opposite of what my brother or sister would have done. They would have cried and stayed at home all week, traumatized from the outdoors. That gives you an idea of how different I was. Plus, if you're keeping track here, I'm a middle child. I have a sister who's three years older and a brother who's six years younger. That middle child syndrome is real. I was the black sheep of the family in every sense of the phrase.

Every Friday, we would have special nights where my dad would pick up a bucket of KFC, a pizza from Pizza Inn, or McDonald's. It's funny to me now, because I can't believe we used to eat all this fast food every Friday. It was a treat, especially the Happy Meals with the prizes inside! We didn't have many options... either super fancy restaurants or fast food. There really weren't that many in-between options. Let me also add that we Indians will barter the shit out of anything if you give us a chance. We are *super* frugal. You know what I'm saying? So, that's what we do.

My mom and dad, God bless them, brought us here to the States to have a better life. And I gave them nothing but trouble with my independent, social, outgoing attitude. I kind of wanted to be more of an American than an Indian. I laugh about it now, but I put my poor parents through so much trauma. I'm so sorry, Mom and Dad!

Eventually, we got to a point where my mom convinced my dad to start bringing all of his family over from India so we'd have company and they could live the American Dream, too. She also wanted to bring her sister over from India. My mom only has one sister, but my dad has two sisters and four brothers. My mom's side of the family is from Rajasthan, and my dad's side is from Punjab. So, gradually, they started the visa process, and man, let me tell you, once they started arriving, it was absolutely insane because I became the unofficial leader of all of my cousins since I was older than all of them.

So, here's the family tree. You have my dad. He's the eldest. There's a sister after him, and then he has four younger brothers and another sister. The two brothers right after my dad had three kids each. The other two brothers had two kids each. Eventually, I would become the leader of the entire crazy bunch, but right now, I was the leader of the few cousins who came immediately from India because the others weren't born yet. To be clear, my sister didn't want to have anything to do with little kids, so watching and entertaining them became my responsibility. My sister loved hanging out with all of the adults, the aunties, moms, and elders because she was kind of prim and proper and preferred mature company. I loved it, though, because I got to control everybody. I was the leader and got to tell everybody what to do. Who wouldn't want to be the boss? I felt like I was their teacher. I also loved pretend play, and my imagination was wild! So, of course, I was happy with leading the kids and having fun with them.

But going back to the regular family dynamic, my brother and I had so much fun together over the years. Yes, we fought all the time. Of course, we did. But with him, I got to do things that I didn't get to do with my sister: play with cars, video games, and stuff like that. It wasn't until later on in life that we got a Super Nintendo, and oh, my God, the stories from that time. We had so much fun playing video games and listening to music, and I absolutely LOVED playing cars with him. We would watch the coolest cartoons together, too. We got into *Voltron* and anime. We would watch *Speed Racer*, *Transformers*, *Sesame Street*, and *The Electric Company*. OMG! I fucking loved *The Electric Company*!! The Flintstones, Tom & Jerry, Woody Woodpecker, Bugs Bunny, Scooby-Doo. I loved watching *Good Times*! That was one of my favorite shows! And *The Jeffersons*? The best!

When my cousins started coming from India, they joined the mix, too, because they were around the same age as my brother. After they stayed with us for a few months to get situated, they'd finally go off on their own and lived in their own apartments.

The adults also put me in charge of taking the kids to the pool. I was maybe nine or ten years old and watching over five- to seven-year-olds! Keep in mind that there were no lifeguards. There was no safety at this point. To make matters worse, I had failed swimming TWICE at the YMCA. I was an underwater swimmer, and my mom tried to get my sister and me to learn how to swim. Both of us failed miserably. Basically, we were not good at it. I mean, at one point, I cracked my chin on the concrete edge of the pool. I don't even remember how old I was, maybe six or seven years old. Showing off to the other kids. Then I jumped backward into the pool, my chin hit the edge, and I slid in slowly. I ended up getting three stitches because of that. My mom tells this story to people, too, and emphasizes that I didn't cry once while getting stitches. I was gangsta like that. But seriously, I can't believe they would allow me to watch their kids in the pool when I had zero training or life-saving abilities. I couldn't even save myself, much less these kids, if anything were to happen. Thankfully, nothing bad ever happened under my watch.

We loved living in our house. And of all the street names to get when you're a kid growing up, we lived on Apothecary Lane. I don't know if you've ever heard the word "apothecary." You probably have, but never imagined it being a street name. That was a bitch to spell! And that was my street forever! We had the absolute time of our lives there, living our American Dream. That's what everybody wants to do when they come from India and live in America, which was one of the reasons that my mom wanted my dad's family and her own sister and her family to come and be with us: to share in the dream. The grandparents started coming as well. My mom's parents came first. My mom's dad, my nanaji, basically grew up in Rajasthan, India, under British rule. He had the most impeccable English and could play chess like a champ.

And let me tell you, he used to get so frustrated with me, my sister, and my brother, asking us, "Why do you always speak in this slang? Why can't you speak proper English?" He would sit us down and give us speeches like nobody's business. My dad and several other Sikh elders in the community got together and started a Sikh Gurdwara (temple) in Houston, and my grandfather loved giving speeches! Oh, my gosh, everyone knew that when he got up to give a speech, it was going to be a *loooooong* time before he was done. Give yourself a solid hour or two and relax. Granted, he was a brilliant speaker, but man, he would drone on and on. It was both beautiful and frustrating. Whenever I would get stuck having a conversation with Saji (that's what we lovingly called him), all I could think was, *I need to get out of here. Somebody save me.* But it was the cutest thing. My sister and brother would get caught in long conversations with him more than I would because I was incredibly clever and would find a way out.

My grandmother, my nani, gosh, Saji loved her so much! It's very rare to see that type of relationship in my culture. We would find out later in life, after getting access to his journals and diaries, that he would write poems and beautiful notes about her, just memories about her. It was so sweet! Their relationship was so special. She was the first grandparent that I lost. She died very peacefully in 1982, and my grandfather was devastated. Her death was very difficult because I'd never seen a dead body, funeral home, or cremation before. HOLY SHIT! The cremation terrified me! I kept thinking that she was in the oven and feeling the heat and fire. It was really scary. I was only 11 years old. Death scared the crap out of me.

Later that year, we went on our first family vacation to Disney World to celebrate my brother's fifth birthday. It was a trip like no other – you won't get something like that in this day and age. We all got into our 1976 Cutlass Supreme. The car was the exact same age as my brother – my dad got it when my brother was born – and we packed that jalopy up and went to Disney World. We drove all the way. My brother, sister, and I sat in the backseat with no seatbelts because we were gangsta back in the day. We fought the whole way, but we had an amazing time. Back then, it was just Magic Kingdom. They didn't have a bajillion parks. If I remember correctly, Epcot was being built during that time, but it wouldn't open until either later that year or the following year. We also went to some weird wax museum, picked fresh oranges, and ate at Stuckey's on the way there and on the way back. That was the BEST!

We did a bunch of traditional Indian things, too. We would go to the Indian stores, rent Bollywood movies, and come home and watch them. I loved those movies more for the songs and dancing than the storylines. At some point, I don't remember if it was 1978 or 79, VCRs came out, and man, that was a game changer. We would bring home the newest Bollywood movies, borrow a second VCR from an uncle, connect both VCRs and start ripping those videos. We had our whole system down pat so we could watch those movies over and over and over again. It became a family tradition. We had lots of family members, and everyone needed their own copy of *Satte Pe Satta*. It was absolutely hilarious.

We also watched regular TV. My mom was addicted to *All My Children*. There I was, this elementary kid, watching *All My Children* on the days that I had off from school. Sometimes, my mom would let both my sister and me watch, but other times, she would send me out of the room. I was like, "I want to watch it, too!" But I was three years younger than my sister, and the show did have some adult content back then.

It might have been problematic for me to watch *All My Children*, but it still shocks me to this day that at the age of nine and ten, we were allowed to watch *Psycho* and *The Exorcist*. After watching them, we'd say to one another, "Oh, my God! So scary!" and then we would try to go to sleep. My sister and I shared a bedroom, each of us with a twin bed, while my brother had his own bedroom. My sister and I would push those two twin beds together and turn the lights on, and we'd leave them on all night long because we were terrified of these horror movies, and I WAS NINE! I did not want to be the person who slept on the side of the bed that was not by the wall because I needed protection. But I also wanted to protect my sister, so sometimes, I would be the one sleeping on the end of the bed. We did have that one thing in common: My sister and I loved watching scary movies, even though they terrified the crap out of us at such a young age.

We would go to Gurdwara, too. I loved going because that's where my best friend and I would meet up every Sunday. She and her family lived in a badass house in the Memorial area of Houston. We would listen to the Saturday Night Fever soundtrack on a loop! She was the only friend with whom I was allowed to have sleepovers because my mom knew her parents. Even then, I only got to sleep over at her house maybe two or three times before my mom put the kibosh on it, saying, "No more sleepovers. That's an American thing, and we don't do stuff like that."

I wanted to rebel a little bit here and there, but at the end of the day, I was like, *It is what it is.* I think about it sometimes, but I realize that my parents didn't know any better. They were only doing what they thought was right, which, at the time, was for me to not have sleepovers and not do the things that American kids were doing. Plus, my sister didn't really care for those things, so my parents felt it would be in my best interest to follow her lead. The situation became very interesting, though, as I started to wonder, *How am I supposed to act? My sister and I are total opposites, and if we're here in America and are already doing American things like eating meat, then why can't I do more American things?*

A little background about the Sikh religion: You're not supposed to cut your hair, men wear turbans (some women do as well), and you're not supposed to eat meat, drink alcohol, or do drugs. So, the meat thing was weird… were we supposed to or not supposed to? Honestly, the diet thing probably played a pivotal role in my failing health later in life; I just didn't know it then. I didn't know that all of the bologna and hot dogs I was consuming were so harmful to me. I never once thought, "Hey, maybe you shouldn't be eating all this processed food."

I loved bologna and hot dogs. That was the type of stuff I took to school for lunch, so it became very challenging. I was eating school lunches, too, and being introduced to foods that I had never heard of, like chicken fried steak and burritos. OMG, I was in American food heaven!

CHAPTER 2
ROSY/JASMINDER/JASI/JAZZY/JASMINE

BEFORE WE DROWN
Depeche Mode

We must stand up in order to fall down, right?
Falling down is fine, but...
Why must we feel like we are drowning at times?

Now my identity crisis really started to set in. Seriously. If anybody had an identity crisis, it was me. I had no idea who I was. I felt like I knew who I was, but then I would go to school and become a totally different person than I was at home. I was Rosy at home and Jasminder at school. I was really going through a major who-the-fuck-am-I moment. I got to be more independent, open, loud, and fun. I got to speak my piece more. I got to talk about feelings. I got to be the outrageously outspoken extrovert that I was.

I would try my best to convince my mom to let me wear my hair open. She would never let me wear it open completely, but I thought that if I could just do a ponytail on top with a rubber band but have my hair open every once in a while, she would allow me to do that. It just made my day because it was all about compromises at this point. And picture day was one of those days!

She would allow me to wear my hair down on picture days! Sikhs don't cut their hair, so the girls wear it in braids or a bun for modesty.

It wasn't until I started getting a little bit older that my mom said, "Okay, you're not a little kid anymore. You need to have your hair in a braid because you're not supposed to wear it open until you get married, and your husband says it's okay." Whaaaaaaaat? I know, cringe, right? Okay, I get it. But I didn't really know all of those things before, either. To me, it was like, okay, well, someday, I would like to have a husband and a married life and maybe a kid of my own and live the dream that every girl has, be homely and shit. But I still never really thought about things like that. I never gave much thought to that whole stereotypical husband and kids and a home life. If I did think about those things, they weren't at the top of my mind. My girlfriends would talk about planning their own weddings, like, "Oh, I've been planning my wedding since I was three, and I have my dress picked out," but that was not me. I was more of a tomboyish type. I would rather play outside, be on my bike, hang out with my friends, or draw and dance.

Dancing and music were my absolute life! Any chance I got to have the radio on, I would turn it on. I had some confusion with that, too. I liked disco. It was my absolute jam, like Diana Ross and Donna Summer. My very first record was a Debbie Boone album, *You Light Up My Life*. I think my sister had gotten that record. As far as I was concerned, everything that was hers was mine, too. Being three years younger, I always got the hand-me-downs anyway. Then we got "Disco Duck," and oh, that disco jam "The Fifth of Beethoven" was the absolute best. I used to dance and sing to that record all the time! My sister would even dance with me sometimes, and let me tell you – she's going to KILL ME for saying this, *buuuuuuut* – I have video proof that my sister could do the robot like nobody's business! She did a mean robot!

In elementary school, we used to do square dancing. Maybe that was just a Texas thing. We used to do it around rodeo season. They would partner you up, or you would pick a partner. Then we would have a massive square dance with the entire grade level. My parents were not very happy about that because they were partnering the girls up with the boys. I was not allowed to be partnered with boys, which I was kind of okay with. I liked to dance, but I didn't want to dance with boys. They were gross and stinky. The downside was that not participating drew unwanted attention to me. "Why doesn't she have to do it? What makes her so special?"

I also wasn't allowed to pass out Valentine's Day cards to the boys in my class. I remember going to school just crushed on Valentine's Day, thinking, *Oh, God, all the boys are going to hate me now because I can't give them any cards. I can only give cards to the girls.* I would try to get there early enough to put cards into the bags before anybody could notice. Some of the boys would come up and say, "You don't have a card for me, do you?"

"No, I'm sorry," I'd reply.

"Well," they'd say, "Then I'm not giving you my card either," and it just became a whole thing. Ugh. It was traumatic.

Poor me, having to deal with this shit. I'm so sorry, baby! This is the older, wiser me talking to the younger me. Boo, I'm so sorry you had to go through this because that was tough.

I don't know what my parents were afraid of. It was elementary school. They were just kids like me; what did they think was going to happen? I laugh about it now, especially since my brother was allowed to give cards to girls when he was in school. Oh, well. Again, trying to find the humor in the situation is very beneficial and has always been the best thing for me. That's always been my coping mechanism.

There was one thing that annoyed me about school – and about racism in general because, yes, it's very real. Because I was the only Indian kid in my class, before Thanksgiving, I would become an honorary Native American. Well, they didn't say Native American back then. All the white and non-Indian kids got to be the cowboys, and I was the only Indian, so I got to wear the feather. Yes, it's as humorous as it sounds, but it was awful back then. This happened on a yearly basis. It was so stupid and so humiliating. But what are you going to do? I was also so fucking confused by American Indians being called Indian because they were from here, and I was from the opposite side of the world. How was it possible? I was *sooooo* confused. I thought, *If I'm Indian and they are Indian, surely we are related?* OMG. It wasn't until junior high that it finally hit me. Fucking Christopher Columbus and his dumb ass.

I remember my parents would get so frustrated when I would come home with those stupid feathers. No offense to my Native American readers. I'm sure you are equally annoyed by ignorant people linking Indians to your beautiful, TRUE American heritage. If anyone is an "American," it's YOU! YOU were here first! No one else has that right. People are ignorant, and we now know that the history that we've been taught isn't all legit. My parents would ask me, "Surely, they DO know that you're not that kind of Indian, right?" At a certain point, you just throw your hands up and let it go. If you can't beat them, join them, right? That was how I thought about it at the time. I was always struggling to fit in, struggling to figure out who the real me was. Was the real me at home, religious, going to Gurdwara every Sunday, or was it hanging out with my friends after school, riding bikes, and just being the person I was in school? It was very difficult to decide.

One day, I got the lead role in our school play. Everyone auditioned. I mean that in the loosest sense of the term. It was elementary school, you know what I'm saying? So, it wasn't like we were in a theater program or something. It was a Halloween play, and I got the lead role as the witch. To this day, I don't know if that was a racist thing or not. I'll be honest with you. I mean, do I like to act? Yes. Am I good at it? Yes. But do I think I should have gotten that role? I don't know. Maybe they gave me the part because I had witch-like hair, or maybe it was because I was brown. I don't know if it was a racist thing or not, but I did get the role.

My parents were not happy with it, though. "They chose you to be a WITCH? Hell, no!" My mom wouldn't allow it. I was very upset that I did not get to do that role, but I also understood where my parents were coming from. Alas, my theatrical debut would have to wait. I think it's important to say that I'm not sharing these things about my parents to make it sound as though I hold any type of grudge toward them. Yeah, I wish they had been a little bit more lenient with me, but they did what they thought was right because my sister was very introverted, and she never really wanted to do fun things. She never really wanted to do sleepovers, play outside, or hang out with friends. She was very book-smart, and I was the exact opposite.

So, my parents didn't know what the hell to do with me. Let's just put it that way. My parents didn't know how to rein me in and bring me back. I'm over here slapping my hands, trying to make a point. THEY DID NOT KNOW HOW TO REIN ME IN. I was all over the place, and I loved it. I loved being active. I loved being out there and creative, and I was always dancing.

One day, my family and I were shopping at Kmart, and we saw a huge display for Michael Jackson's *Thriller*. Oh, my God, I lost my damn mind! I BEGGED my parents for that cassette, and it helped that my brother and sister were fans, too. I was so excited when we got that cassette. I would dance to his songs. I mean, you don't understand. THE ENTIRE ALBUM WAS FIRE. We would have family parties all the time, family get-togethers, and dinner parties, and there were times when that was my highlight. I would put on the *Thriller* cassette and just start dancing in front of all my aunts and the other kids. It was the funniest thing. My sister and I would both put on shows! She would dance to Indian music, Bollywood songs, and I would dance to Michael Jackson because that was my jam, and I was pretty damn good at it, too! More importantly, I loved it. I was having the time of my life!

There was a point in third grade where I would get into the most trouble in my life. My parents were very cautious with the money that we spent. We were very frugal. And they weren't huge fans of wasting money on frivolous things. One of my friends had this really cute little toy. All the little kids loved them. It was a little animal where, if you pinched its back, its arms would open. It was like a clip that you could attach to your papers, notebook, or bag. We didn't have backpacks back then. We just carried all of our books, which is ridiculous. But anyway, my friend had one of these little animal thingies, and I wanted one, too.

I knew I wasn't allowed to have one because they were frivolous and not something that warranted spending money on. So, I stole it – and I got caught! It was like the Jane's Addiction song "Been Caught Stealing," right? "I've been caught stealing once when I was five," but I wasn't five; I was nine. They had to call my mom. I got into *sooooo* much trouble. The teachers were so disgusted with my behavior that they put me in the library to wait for my mom. My mom came and picked me up, and I knew I was in trouble because she didn't say SHIT in the car on the way home.

My sister, my brother, and I all wore glasses, and we KNEW we were in trouble the moment my mom would say, "Take your glasses off" because that meant that we were about to get it. She was not about to ruin the glasses that we paid good money for. So we would take them off before getting a spanking. OMG! I crack up about this now because it's so hilarious! Why? Because I rarely got an ass-whooping. Usually, I was clever enough to get out of it. I would book it, running from my mom, but my brother and sister were the type of kids who just sat around and took the beating. They were like, "Okay, fine. I did something wrong. Give me my beating." Not me, man. I was like, "Nope. I'm out. That is not how I do things." I would book it! After a while, my mom would forget that she was upset with me and just let it go because she couldn't stop laughing.

It's funnier now than it ever was back then, but that's how I dealt with things. That's just who I was. That's the person I've always been inside, and it's absolutely hilarious. If there was a loophole or a way to save my ass, you better believe I was going to find it. And please don't get me wrong. My parents WERE NOT abusive. We kids simply got punished for things that we were not supposed to do. There were repercussions for our actions.

At the end of each school year, we had something called field day, and I loved it. Y'all remember those? I absolutely loved field day. Why? Because I was a fast runner. In the fourth grade, I was one of the fastest runners in my class, and field day that year was absolutely amazing. But then something happened: They opened up a new elementary school. To do this, they had to split up the current elementary schools, so they sent a letter home to everybody. I had been with the same group of kids since kindergarten. The letter said that if you had a sibling who was going to be starting school – which I did because my brother would be starting kindergarten – you would be zoned to a different school. You could get out of it by having your parents sign a letter keeping you in your current school, but then I would have gone to one school while my brother went to another, and that would not have been good.

Even though I wanted to stay with my friends and not go to another school, I knew I couldn't. I realized later in life that my parents had to send us to the exact same school because we had to take the same bus anyway. I got zoned to this other school, and my brother and I were enrolled. Oh, boy. That was when the drama started. This school was in a very affluent area in Houston. I would say it was 99% white – and not just white but stupid rich and entitled. I hit the quota for the one Indian person in my fifth grade. Keep in mind that my family is traditional Sikh, so my brother had a small turban called a patka for a young boy. Bullied much? It was awful for him. He has his own story to tell, and maybe, one of these days, he'll share it with the world, too.

Boy, I had no idea that bullying was going to get me, too. My dad got bullied and made fun of for his turban, we got made fun of when we wore our traditional Indian salwar kameez in public, and my brother got bullied for wearing his patka. But me? I'd seemed to coast from kindergarten to fourth grade without major incident. Yeah, people would make fun of me here and there for having braids and whatever, but it wasn't relentless the way that it was in fifth grade. In fifth grade, these assholes would NOT STOP. They were absolutely relentless and ruthless, constantly calling me names and telling me I smelled and was gross and nasty. They made fun of my braids. I thought, *Gosh, you're so ignorant,* but I brushed it off and tried to go about my day.

Bullying was not the massive thing back then that it is now. Nowadays, if you see something, you say something. That really didn't happen back then. I think it took me the whole first semester before I even said anything to my mom because I was terrified. I was also terrified of going to school because these kids would not fucking stop. The most hurtful thing about this whole situation was that none of the kids that I'd grown up with from kindergarten through fourth grade who transferred to the same school tried to stop the bullying. Nobody said, "Hey, leave her the fuck alone." And some of them were my FRIENDS. It took me a REALLY long time to finally confess to my mom that the kids were bullying me. She came to the school, and we talked with the counselor. Nothing changed. No one was reprimanded. The bullying never stopped. I didn't have a lot of hope that it would stop because it never stopped for my brother, either. It was brutal.

And do you know what else was also happening at that time? That's right! Puberty, ladies and gentlemen. Bodily changes were happening. So, what do I mean by that? You start to stink. Your pits start to stink. And for Indian people, yes, I'm going there. I don't know if we just get it earlier because we're Indian. I know what all the jokes are, but I got major stinky pits. So, on top of having to have my hair up in braids all the time, I had stinky pits, too.

My mom, bless her heart, sold Avon – and Tupperware, but we're talking about Avon right now. This is truly funny, though it didn't seem so much back then. Instead of going to the grocery store or Eckerd Drugs, Walgreens, or another drug store, instead of getting Secret or Ban or any other of the big deodorant brands back then, instead of getting a REAL deodorant, my mom gave me one from Avon. It was fine and perfumy, but it was one of those roll-ons. They were the big thing back then. I don't know if you've ever used a roll-on deodorant before, especially as a fifth-grade kid when you are sweating *a lot,* but that shit drips, so I had pit stains on my shirts. To make matters worse, it was more like a perfume for your pits than a deodorant-antiperspirant. It worked, but it also didn't work, you know what I mean? Basically, it didn't really solve my issue. But even after I finally did get a hold of real deodorant, they still bullied me for stinking when they knew damn well I no longer stank. Assholes.

Needless to say, that year was absolutely miserable for me as far as bullying was concerned, and I was just done with it. Looking back on it now, it was so stupid, and I wish I would have ignored them more and not internalized so much of the pain. I was so grateful that the school year was coming to a close, and what happens at the end of the year? You guessed it: my favorite day, field day.

So, field day arrives, and because my hormones are going crazy and I'm stinky pits, guess what else is happening at that same time? I got a lot of hair growing, and I mean A LOT of hair growing, and my legs are HAIRY "AF." On field day, am I supposed to wear shorts? I don't think so. Call me Sasquatch because it was a struggle! So, I brought it up to my mom and said, "Didi" – Didi is a respectful Indian term for your older sister – "Didi's shaving her legs. Can I shave mine? I have a field day coming up."

"No," she said, "you can't shave your legs until you're in the sixth grade."

"Well, sixth grade is going to happen in a few months. Can I please just start early?"

"Nope, you gotta figure it out. Wear some pantyhose. It'll be okay."

Shit! Okay, so we get some pantyhose, and I put it on, and I'm like, huh? OMG. So, I don't know if you've ever put pantyhose on over incredibly hairy legs. My sister and I basically got my dad's hairy DNA, but my mom's practically hairless. She really is. My sister and I have always been incredibly jealous of the fact that she has zero hair on her entire body. We're just like, "Dang it, man, why did we have to go to Dad on this one thing?" LOL. But if you've never worn pantyhose over a leg with a shit ton of hair, all it does is allow the hairs to pop out of the pantyhose. THEY'RE STILL THERE, AND YOU CAN STILL SEE THEM. In fact, they're almost magnified at this point because the hose gives a sheer sheen to your legs, and you have hairs poking out. I don't know what I was expecting to happen. I suppose I thought the pantyhose would magically cover the hair. Y'ALL... seriously.

So, I was like, "Well, damn. I'm just going to have to go with it. My mom's not going to let me shave my legs. This is my only option. I'm just going to go with the flow." And I kid you not, I went to field day and was like, *I guess this is how I'm going out at this school!* Anyway, no one said anything. Weird, right? NO ONE made fun of me that day. Not sure why. But I could hear laughing and snickering. They had a boombox and were playing music while the track and field portion was happening during field day. I asked if they could play Blondie's "Rapture" during my leg of the run. It was a baton race, and I was the final runner.

And let me tell you something, my dear reader! When these assholes who made so much fun of me realized that I'd won the race and our grade had ended up winning the whole field day, it was a beautiful moment, and I instantly became "normal" and acceptable in their eyes. All I could think was, *Where the fuck were you guys this entire year? Why were you so mean to me? Why were you making fun of my braids and stuff, and look who came through for you at the tail end? Assholes.*

Anyway, I spent way too much time on that part of my story, but I didn't realize until much later in life that the trauma associated with that bullying, along with internalizing the pain and the confusion of my identity crisis, would contribute to my health issues later on. Studies have shown that stress, especially from a prolonged traumatic event, can quite literally make a person sick, and that could have been something that contributed to my issues.

Aw, look at sweet little me getting to wear my hair down for my 5th grade picture day!

Well, I was so excited to get out of that school and to start junior high and finally see some of my older friends who hadn't screwed me over in fifth grade. Sadly, I didn't realize that when I got into junior high, into the sixth grade, I was walking directly into the path of yet another bullying nightmare.

I met these girls on my bus, two white girls, and they were so mean to me. They wanted to be "friends" with me, and they were both double my size.

I never tried to say anything to them. I never tried to fight with them. I never tried to do anything because I thought, *They will kick my ass. There's no doubt about it. They will kick my ass.* They would get on the bus and call me "JazzArabianIndian," all of it together. Yes, I know it's stupid now, but then I was fucking terrified! I guess they thought that saying these things would make me angry, and I would try to fight them or cry or whatever. It didn't. They also called me Jasminder Fender Bender. Okay, that one is hilarious! Not back then, but TODAY! That one cracks me up! It was so stupidly funny! But they were terrifying! They just scared me. They scared me more than anything else. So, I tried to laugh it off and make jokes so that they could see that I was fun. I was like, "Ha, ha, yeah, good joke. That was a good one. Yeah, you got me good that time. Y'all are so badass." And yes, I still tried to be "friends" with them because I was terrified of them and did not want them to screw me over. Keep your enemies close, right? Isn't that the saying? They had stolen my lunch money before. They had taken other things from me, too, like pens, pencils, and other supplies.

There were moments when it was simply too much to bear, and I would walk away from them. I would sit in the front of the bus by the driver, but they would still bully me. The bus driver wouldn't say a damn thing. It just became another never-ending cycle of pain and peer pressure. The two girls smoked cigarettes at the bus stop and after school, and they constantly tried to get me to do it, too. Smoking was still allowed in high schools at that time!

The saddest part about the bullying in sixth grade is that I started talking to some of the people who had bullied me in fifth grade, and they started looking up to me. Why were they looking up to me? Because I started bullying other people, too. I know! It was AWFUL! If I knew you in the sixth grade and I bullied you, I am so sorry. I am so sorry because it was so stupid and so obnoxious. The way that I dealt with the bullying was by passing the torch, paying it forward, and doing it to somebody else. I said some mean and hurtful things to one person in particular. I do not remember her name, but I swear to God that if I ever do remember who this person is, I will track them down, give them the biggest hug, say, "I'm so sorry, and I was so stupid," and beg for their forgiveness. I just didn't know any better. When you're going through something like that, your brain starts doing things, and you start behaving in ways that you never thought you would.

I never thought that I would be mean like that to anybody else. It's not like I did it relentlessly. I didn't. I only did it a few times, but it was enough to make me disgusted with myself. It was absolutely unacceptable, and I hope I did not destroy that person's life or hurt them in the way that I was being hurt. I can't believe I hurt somebody like that. Bullying is so awful.

I tried to find solace in the things that made me happy, and at that time, it was drawing. I used to make birthday cards, anniversary cards, and general ones like get-well cards for my family. Keep in mind that everyone was in Houston now: my dad and my mom, my siblings and I, and my dad's four brothers. The younger brothers eventually went back to India to get married and started their families once their wives arrived, so there were a lot of us, which meant a lot of birthdays, anniversaries, etc. I stayed busy. I made everybody's cards.

I loved drawing roses and flowers. Honestly, I just love to draw. That was my jam. Not only did I enjoy it, but I was also really good at it. I knew I wouldn't be allowed to pursue it as an actual degree in college because, you know, I'm Indian. If you know anybody who's Indian, Asian, or from any other strict culture, you know that you have four options for your higher education: you're either going to become a doctor (which is the number one choice for my peeps), a lawyer, an engineer, or a businessperson. Those are your four options, and you don't deviate from them. If you do, you better have a REALLY good solution as to how much money you're going to make and have a whole proposal queued up to present your facts because you're going to need that to convince your parents to back you!

At the end of the day, it's all about clout. It's all about who's doing what and where they are going to college. The more Ivy League your school is, the more bragging rights your parents have. That's what it's all about. Yes, they want you to do well. Yes, they want you to have a good salary, but at the end of the day, they want to tell all of their friends about how amazing you are. So, remember that because that'll come back later, too.

That was not what I wanted. I didn't want those four things. There was a short period when I wanted to be a lawyer and would have been REALLY good at it, too, but I was more into the glamor of it and had no intention of doing all that work to get there! I wanted to go into art. I wanted to draw. I wanted to just explore that creative side of me because that was who I was, that was what I wanted, that was what made me happy. I was that wild child.

Like I said, I don't blame my parents. I actually feel bad for what I put my parents through. I really, really do because I just wanted them to understand me and see where I was coming from, to let me be who I am. This is who I am. This is who I feel that I am. Please love me for who I am. This is me. Please let me be me. But it was really hard for me to express myself to my parents. They didn't take me seriously. I was told to simply be more like my sister. But I wasn't.

CHAPTER 3

TELL ME WHY

BLASPHEMOUS RUMORS

Depeche Mode

The first time I heard this song, I cried like a baby.
It was speaking DIRECTLY to me.
Why does it seem like God has a sick sense of humor?
Why am I going through this?
Why do I feel as though He'll be laughing at me,
or perhaps WITH me, when I die?

T his chapter is pretty intense because it sets the stage for what's about to happen in my life that will change the course of everything. Thus far, I have set the foundation for how rambunctious, extroverted, crazy, happy, full of life, and energetic I was, constantly dancing, drawing, and playing sports. I don't believe I mentioned this, but I made the first cut on the basketball and volleyball teams in sixth grade. However, my parents didn't want me to play on a team for school, so I wasn't allowed to do that. This was fine because it would have been a lot of responsibility, but I did make it that far.

Basketball, volleyball, soccer, gymnastics, running, track, you name it – I excelled at it. I loved it. The only sport that I couldn't seem to get a hold of was swimming. Remember the movie *Bend It Like Beckham*? The main character is my namesake, Jasminder, and she's struggling to find herself in her strict Sikh family, who doesn't support her love for soccer. Yeah, I felt like that movie was part of my own story.

I have also established my passion for drawing. It was my main thing, and I drew ALL THE TIME! That's why my parents thought it was weird when I started complaining about swelling in my right thumb. It started when I was 13, and it was incredibly painful. My parents said, "You need to stop drawing because it's making your thumb hurt. Stop drawing, and it'll go away." I stopped drawing, but it didn't get better. Instead, my left thumb swelled the same way. At that point, my parents became concerned and called our family doctor. He said, "I don't think it's anything to worry about. Bring her in, and we'll check her out. There's a slight chance it might be arthritis."

My parents brought me in, and the blood work was done. When the results came back, the doctor said, "She has rheumatoid arthritis. You need to have her checked out at Texas Children's Hospital in the pediatric rheumatology department."

To remind you, little me, little Rosy, was the black sheep of the family, so when I heard this news about having a disease, I was like, *Oh, wait, there's something wrong with me? Soooooo, am I going to get attention now?* I kind of liked it. I had heard the term "arthritis" before – or, as they say in Texas, "ARTHUR-it-is" – but only in the context of grandparents and other elderly folks, so that's what I likened it to.

We went to Texas Children's Hospital, where more blood work was done. When the results came back, sure enough, I had polyarticular juvenile rheumatoid arthritis. Keep in mind that the year was 1984, and there weren't many treatments available. I mean, you could take aspirin or Tylenol, and Naprosyn was the big thing back then, but that was it for treatments.

I started going to Texas Children's Hospital weekly and got the treatments, physical therapy (PT), and occupational therapy (OT). My mom drove me all the way from where we lived to the medical center in Houston, where, thankfully, we have a world-renowned medical center. On these trips, going back and forth to the hospital, I would listen to the radio, and that was when I first heard Depeche Mode. They are still my absolute favorite band of all time. They really are. I didn't realize how much they would help me along my long journey and be so critical in helping me and allowing me to heal my soul.

The very first song I ever heard from them was "People Are People." It used to remind me of my bullying days. Why do people hate each other for no apparent reason?

PEOPLE ARE PEOPLE
Depeche Mode

Why can't people get along sometimes?
Yes, we are different colors and different creeds
and we all have different needs.
Hell, I've never done anything to you.
What did I do wrong?
I simply can't understand what makes someone hate another.
Help me understand.

I heard it traveling back and forth to the Texas Children's Hospital Pediatric Diseases Clinic. I met other kids there who had diabetes, lupus, and other diseases I had never even heard of. I even met a baby who was born with juvenile rheumatoid arthritis (JRA). Holy shit! How awful! That baby would try to stand up in the waiting room, and their tiny knees were so swollen. It was so sad. I don't even think I knew any adults who had some of the diagnoses that I and my fellow chronic pediatric patients had.

I had never even heard of rheumatoid arthritis, only arthritis by itself, and they are *very* different. Straight from the CDC's website:

> *Rheumatoid arthritis, or RA, is an autoimmune and inflammatory disease, which means that your immune system attacks healthy cells in your body by mistake, causing inflammation (painful swelling) in the affected parts of the body. RA mainly attacks the joints, usually many joints at once. RA commonly affects joints in the hands, wrists, and knees. In a joint with RA, the lining of the joint becomes inflamed, causing damage to joint tissue. This tissue damage can cause long-lasting or chronic pain, unsteadiness (lack of balance), and deformity (misshapenness). RA can also affect other parts of the body and cause problems in organs such as the lungs, heart, and eyes. What causes RA? RA occurs when the body's immune system attacks its own healthy cells. The specific causes of RA are unknown, but some factors can increase the risk of developing the disease (Source: CDC website).*

I didn't know what was happening to me. I just knew that I didn't like the pain and swelling parts of it, but I loved the attention. Every time I left the doctor's office, my mom would take me to Del Taco, which was my favorite taco place, to get my favorite burrito, or stop by McDonald's or just someplace where I could get a treat afterward, maybe an ice cream sundae or apple pie. I don't know about you, but I live for positive reinforcement, fun, and excitement! It gave me something to mask the pain a bit and something to look forward to.

I liked the attention I was getting from my parents AND my siblings. My brother and sister were told to be VERY careful with me and that I was fragile now. Did I abuse this power? Why, yes, I did. LOL. But I gradually got to a point where I was like, *Okay, this was all fun in the beginning, but I'm not happy about this, and it's really fucking painful.* By listening to music back and forth on those trips, I was able to keep my sanity. I would close my eyes and shut my brain down. Then, I would visualize myself at a DM concert or transport myself to a place where I was dancing freely. It was my peace. It was my solace. My mind and imagination were my escape.

My dad was a senior mechanical engineer, and he got laid off every few years or so when projects would come to an end. So, just before I got diagnosed with JRA, we moved out of our house on Apothecary Lane and headed to Sugar Land. My dad would commute back and forth to Bay City for his job at the power plant, and I rode the bus. I loved living in Sugar Land. It was a totally different environment. Plus, it also got me out of the bullying environment that I'd been in during the fifth and sixth grades. I didn't see any of those kids anymore. I met a whole new set of friends in the seventh and eighth grades in Sugar Land, but that was also where I was diagnosed. I loved living out there. I loved being a part of that community; it was just very different. And it was weird because there were more Indians and diversity in Sugar Land than in Cy Fair, where we used to live. It was kind of neat being around more Indian people out in Sugar Land.

Anyway, I got the diagnosis, and we were going back and forth for my treatments, and I'm progressively getting worse. I was diagnosed in April of 1984, and if you see pictures of me from that point on, when I turned 14 and going into 1985, I was emaciated. I really was. I lost a ton of weight. I was already super skinny, to begin with, and I was hurting so bad and was so swollen. I was having a difficult time moving, eating, and doing daily activities. It's an autoimmune disease. Your body is fighting itself FOR NO REASON. It's like a fucking BULLY! It's basically fighting your cartilage and synovial fluid, and my cartilage was just getting destroyed and eaten up by this stupid, meaningless disease.

Again, I have to remind you that there weren't any miraculous treatments around at this time. So, it was no surprise that my doctors told us about an upcoming drug study using gold treatment for rheumatoid arthritis. My parents were like, "Yeah, she's miserable." It was clear how poorly I was doing just two months after my diagnosis. I was in REALLY bad shape, so they said, "Let's get her on this."

This is the only picture I could find during this time of my life. I was soooo skinny, weak, hunched over. Unrecognizable.

Within a year, I was on that treatment. It was a study, so I didn't really know whether I was on the medication or a placebo. To this day, I still have no idea what I was on. But I can tell you this: By the end of the year, I had gotten down to 70 pounds. I don't remember how much I weighed initially, but I'm going to add something here to this story. I didn't know until later in life that my dad was keeping a daily journal. In 2023, I decided to read them just to piece together a timeline of my health struggle and healing journey. He had been keeping diaries from 1962 all the way to 1998, so I read through every single one of them.

What I learned shocked me. I didn't realize that I had gone into that gold study only *two* months after my diagnosis. I didn't realize that within a year, the disease had spread through almost EVERY SINGLE JOINT in my body. I became so incredibly weak. I was completely emaciated. I was 70 pounds. My joints were so swollen, and I was in so much pain that I could barely eat. My jaws hurt so badly that I could barely open my mouth. I would look at myself in the bathroom mirror, and all I saw were bones, a skeleton with swollen joints. It scared the SHIT out of me. Yes, I wanted attention, but I was not happy with the price I had to pay to get it.

My mom would give me liquid foods, and I would drink those Carnation instant breakfasts anytime I felt some sort of hunger. I only drank the chocolate flavor because chocolate was my jam. Chocolate is my favorite when it comes to desserts or anything. I prefer chocolate cakes and chocolate everything. So, I would try to drink those as many times as I could throughout the day. Sometimes, my mom would have to force me to eat things like that just to keep the weight on me so I could function.

I was swollen, miserable, and hunched over from the pain. I could no longer sit on the floor without help (we sit on the floor for Gurdwara). My mom and sister would help me get on and off the floor. I also couldn't ride the bus anymore. To put this in perspective, it's not like we used to wear baggy pants or anything like that. We wore regular straight-leg jeans; even parachute pants weren't that wide. My knees were so swollen that even with the Indian dress, which is called a salwar kameez and is very wide, I couldn't even get it past my knees! That was how swollen my knees were. And the pain was excruciating! I was so swollen that I couldn't bend my knees or straighten my legs out completely either. If something barely touched them, I would scream bloody murder. It was so incredibly painful that I felt like I was dying, and I had a very difficult time sleeping. I couldn't move in my bed.

My mom would sleep on the twin bed next to me, and every time she would wake up, she would flip me. She would turn me to one side and then go back to sleep. Then, 30 minutes later, an hour later, whenever she would get up again, she would flip me over to the other side. I couldn't move myself. If I woke up, reality would hit, and I would realize my whole body was in extreme pain. Sometimes, I would wail out and start crying, "Mommy, Mommy, please move me," because the pain was so bad. If I slept too long in one position, I couldn't move on that side anymore.

It's very difficult to explain or put into perspective the sheer amount of pain and level of swelling. My body was all bones! Where was this swelling coming from? All you could see were my swollen joints. I would stare at my body in the bathroom mirror, and it was so fucking scary! Who was this emaciated, swollen person staring back at me? My ribs and collarbones jutted out. I was terrified of the person staring back at me from the mirror. What had I done to deserve this? Why was this happening to me? All I could do was cry.

The doctors had me in occupational therapy as my hands were starting to become deformed. If you search on Google for "rheumatoid arthritis" and look at pictures, you'll see deformed hands and fingers that veer off to the sides. Put your left hand down on a flat surface and look at it. Your fingers are straight. With JRA/RA, your fingers start to veer off to the left, and your wrist also curves off to the left. If you're looking at your right hand, your fingers and wrist go off to the right. To keep that from happening, they created splints for me. The best time to wear those splints was at night. I was already so swollen and in so much pain and had so much morning stiffness! When I would put those braces on, I would get up the next morning in the most excruciating pain you could imagine because I wasn't able to move my wrist all night long. Any slight movement in the morning KILLED me.

I don't know how much I cried in 1984 or 1985, but apparently, my tears were limitless, and I felt that no one was listening. I felt like I was completely alone. I know I had 100% support from my parents and siblings, but I felt alone. No one understood the extent of the pain. They were also helpless. I couldn't put it into words. I just wanted to die.

I don't even know how I was able to brush my teeth. I don't know how I was able to take a bath. I don't have a lot of memories from that time, or I'm certain that they are buried DEEP away to save me from what I went through. I'm pretty certain that my mom had to help me with daily functioning. The trauma was INSANE. I was like, *Please just take me now. Just please let me go and put me out of this misery. I don't know what the fuck this is. I'm sorry. I'm sorry if I hurt anybody. I'm sorry if I did anything wrong.*

It's important to remember that I was growing up in a very traditional Indian culture where people said things that they truly should never, ever say out loud, especially to a CHILD. I heard people saying things behind my back and also to my face: "Wow, what did she do to deserve this?" "She's such a pretty girl. It's so unfortunate." "She's never going to get married." "Who's

SAVED BY DEPECHE MODE

ever going to want her like this?" "Why is she suffering like this?" "What did you do as a child?" (I WAS STILL A CHILD.) "What did you do that was so bad that you have the wrath of God on you right now?" Oh, and my favorite, "Nazzar Laggi," which, loosely translated, means, "She was cursed."

As shocking as that sounds, people said that to me to my face… and it wasn't just random people; it was also people in my extended family and close family friends. My inner child is still traumatized every time those memories fill my mind, and my healed, goddess, current self is like, *Are you serious right now? Are you really saying that to a 13-year-old child? How dare you say something like that TO A CHILD! Do you not see what my parents are going through? Watching their child suffering, and you're saying shit like this? How dare you! I can't imagine if my child was struggling with a disease and somebody said things like that to them. What did you do to deserve this? I would have ANNIHILATED that person! I would have ripped them from limb to limb for saying something like that to my child in front of me, to have that type of disrespect and plain AUDACITY!"*

But that shit happened, and I heard it all the fucking time, and it was disgusting & sickening. And they called me "bechari" all the time, which means "poor girl." It was awful. People can be so cruel. Not necessarily intentionally cruel, but cruel nevertheless.

By this point, the disease had ravaged my body to where I could barely walk. I already couldn't ride the bus anymore because the stairs were too high, and I just couldn't move like that. I could barely climb a five-inch step, much less a massive bus step. So, my mom would drop me off in the mornings and pick me up in the afternoons. I was also trying to get an education at the same time as all of this medical shit. I couldn't walk from class to class; it was too much.

We had a conversation with the school nurse, who gave me a five-minute pass. This pass basically allows a student with a disability to get out five minutes early and use another student's help to carry books or anything else that they're not physically able to carry. So, I had a five-minute pass that gave me extra time to get to my classrooms and also allowed me to avoid a busy hallway. That way, I wouldn't get bumped by accident.

But I simply could not walk, so my mom called the school again, and they came up with a solution with the school administration. They said, "Why don't you have her come to school and stay in the library?" So, that's what I did; I just sat in the library all day.

From the moment school started to the time it ended in the afternoon, I stayed in the library, and my work would be brought to me. In hindsight, that was not the best idea for somebody with swollen joints to be sitting in the same position in a freezing library. Schools are cold, you know; schools have always been cold. I don't know whether I had a sweater or a jacket. Again, I don't remember all of the details anymore. But I sat in the library from morning until afternoon, and by the time I got home, I was in so much pain that I could barely think. I didn't have a choice, though. I had to continue to go to school and follow that routine.

Finally, the doctors said, "Clearly, this study medication isn't working. We need to put her in the hospital." To recap, I was diagnosed in April of '84 with two swollen joints. By April of '85, my condition had gotten to a point where I required hospitalization, and every single joint was affected. I still have that hospital discharge report. It says:

The patient is a 14-year-old Indian female. She presented in March 1984 with polyarthritis. She was started on 8 aspirin a day. She was then switched to Naprosyn with some improvement. She developed worsening arthritis, and in June of 1984, she started the oral gold study. For the past several months, she has had persistent anorexia and a 17 lb. weight loss. For 4 days prior to admission, she had noted fever of 100.2, vomiting, and severe joint pain. Over the past several months, she has had anemia. She was an alert, very thin girl who looked chronically ill. She had severe polyarticular Juvenile Rheumatoid Arthritis. Every joint was affected. She also had nodules on her wrist and in the right palm. Both the Naprosyn and gold study were immediately stopped and a bone marrow biopsy was ordered. She was then started on 60 mg of Prednisone per day.

I only weighed 70 pounds. The rheumatoid riddled my body. And the only way they could bring me back to life again was to pump me up with steroids: prednisone. That would be my first time getting steroids. It seemed a miraculous drug at first, as it worked SUPER FAST, but now I realize how terrible and dangerous that drug was.

I was in the hospital for about a week. They got me to see a therapist, but I basically told the therapist I wasn't interested and got out of there. I was like, "I do not need to talk to anybody right now as I'm sort of preoccupied with staying alive. I'm trying to deal with my shit right now." Therapy was not a big deal back then either, so I didn't feel bad about not seeing her. Do I wish now that I would have done it? Yeah, I do. I think my story would be very different right now if I had started therapy back then when I really needed it. But it wasn't a thing, and I was Indian. We definitely didn't believe in therapy. Lol. So, I said no to the therapist.

Then, they sent me to occupational therapy. They had more splints and stuff for me that were made for not only my hands now but also my feet. The same thing happens to your hands with rheumatoid arthritis; it can also happen to your feet, where they veer off to the sides. They also did a bone marrow biopsy on me. I think I cursed every single doctor who was in the examination room or whatever procedure room they had me in. During the biopsy, they extracted marrow from the inside of my hip bone, and these assholes did *not* put me to sleep for it. I was awake for the entire procedure, and they had me lying on my stomach on this hard, uncomfortable "bed" that was more like a hard examination table because it had the paper cover on it.

I was face down on the paper, screaming and crying for them to stop, that it was hurting me, and they held me down and told me to calm down. By the time they finished with the procedure, the entire paper was DRENCHED with my tears and sweat. It was the most traumatic experience in my life thus far. And every time during that week-long hospital stay, if I saw anybody from that procedure room, I gave them the look of death, like, "Don't you ever fucking look at me or touch me ever again in your life. That was the most horrific thing that you guys did to me!"

Remember how I said that steroids are like a miracle drug? It's because they work SUPER fast! Your swelling disappears, your pain disappears, and your appetite increases like crazy. Once I started the treatment, my appetite came back with a vengeance! I started eating right away, and within a matter of months, I went from 70 to 115 pounds. As you can imagine, putting on that amount of weight as quickly as I did in a matter of months gave me the WORST stretch marks from my hips all the way down to my calves. I still have them to this day. They're all faded now, but that's where they originated. And getting them just destroyed me. I was livid and terrified. I had never had a stretch mark before in my life, and now I was riddled with them. They were red, painful, and horribly itchy; it was just absolutely awful. My only solace at the time was the fact that, for a brief moment in time, I seemed to be free of inflammation and pain, and that was enough. The steroids were helping.

But with prednisone, you're not supposed to be on it for longer than a few months at a time, and then you have to start tapering off. So, you get your "heroic dose," if you will, and then gradually, every two weeks or so, you start decreasing the dose until you're completely off the medication. But by the time you're completely off the medication, you're back to stage one with your symptoms because, while it helps reduce inflammation and pain quickly, it doesn't HEAL it; it simply masks the pain temporarily. That's why it's such a shitty treatment. It gives you a false sense of hope that maybe, just maybe, you're cured. You no longer have to suffer. Remember, there was no other treatment that could help me. We tried all of them, including a study.

I honestly believe that I was not being given the actual gold medication, and that's why the disease riddled my body and spread so fast. I wasn't actually getting treated – I was getting the placebo. Sadly, Western medicine had basically failed me. My parents knew this, and I knew this. There weren't any other treatments, so what were we going to do?

CHAPTER 4

TRY "WALKING" IN MY SHOES

WALKING IN MY SHOES

Depeche Mode

This song came out in 1993. I remember hearing it
for the first time and losing it.
By this point, I'd been put through so much.
So much pain. So much suffering.
I dared anyone to try walking in my shoes, just for a day.
And tell me they would have done things differently.

We decided, "Well, we're Indian. Let's see what we can find on the natural side, on the Ayurvedic side, on the holistic side, on the homeopathic side." And that's when we started looking into Eastern medicine. We started looking into homeopathic stuff and reading books. In one book (I don't remember the name), we read that cod liver oil is supposed to be really good for people with rheumatoid arthritis.

We tried it, and my mom was invested, y'all! So much so that we bought a badass juicer. That amazing woman, bless her heart, woke up at 4 a.m. every morning to freshly juice a room-temperature orange. It had to be room temperature, and so did the cod liver oil. She'd mix them together and bring the concoction to me in bed every morning for I don't even know how long.

My brother and sister used to make fun of me for having to drink that awful drink and to be woken up to take it so early every morning, and then one day, my mom said, "You know what? This is going to be good for the WHOLE family!" Ha-ha-ha-ha! So, the whole family had to do it, too! My brother and sister were like, "Damn, now we have to do it, too?"

My parents had them tested for RA, too. After I got the diagnosis, my parents were scared that maybe the other kids had it. Thankfully, they were fine. Nothing was going on with them. But they also got to experience some of the lovely things that I had to do, and cod liver oil was one of those joyful things.

Then, my dad lost his job. We were presented with a choice: Do we stay in Sugar Land or go back to our other house on Apothecary Lane? We still had that house; we were just renting it out. Ultimately, we decided to go back to the Apothecary house, and I was not happy with that because, remember, that's where I was getting bullied in the fifth and sixth grades. I did NOT want to go back to that environment, especially now that I was sick, had swelling and pain, and was dealing with other things. That was the LAST thing that I needed.

I was very scared to move back, but we did. I started all of these different natural treatments for rheumatoid arthritis. We had to get the house back in order after the renters moved out, ripping out the old carpet and putting in a brand-new one because the people who rented the house had two massive dogs, and they had destroyed the carpet, and it was just kind of gross anyway. So, we ripped up the carpet, re-painted the house, moved in, and then I got ready to go back to school.

Thankfully, when I returned to school, I didn't have any major issues with the old bullies. I saw the two girls who used to bully me in the sixth grade, but they left me alone. It was almost like they didn't know who I was. We just looked different; we had evolved, and we had gotten older and wiser, I guess.

I didn't want to have anything to do with them anyway; I just wanted to start over, and that's how it worked out. So, they left me alone.

My homeopathic treatments were coming from different doctors and contacts in our Indian community. I had some of the craziest restrictions with some of these treatments. There was one where I wasn't allowed to eat any red foods while on the treatment. For two weeks, I took these pellets that you put underneath your tongue and waited until they dissolved. And I was like, *Seriously? I can't eat red foods? Like, what do you mean?* So, I couldn't have any tomato sauce or ketchup. Wait, what? Ketchup? Like, ketchup is my thing, man! Like, I eat ketchup with everything. Like, I even eat ketchup with my French toast. I know it's gross. It's an Indian thing. Not syrup, just plain French toast with glorious ketchup! Lol. I love ketchup with creamy pasta or mac and cheese, ketchup with my fries, ketchup with my burgers, ketchup with my hot dogs, and ketchup with my samosas and pakoras! Oh, man. I mean, ketchup, ketchup, ketchup. I love ketchup.

Also, keep in mind that many Indian foods are made with tomato sauce. So, I don't know if you've ever had an Indian dish called mattar paneer with peas and cheese. That's a very famous Indian/Punjabi dish, and it happened to be one of my favorite dishes at the time. When my mom made it for everybody else, she put tomato sauce in it, but for me, it was green. *GREEEEEEEEEN.*

Let me explain something to you about Indian food. When you add tomato sauce to certain Indian foods, even if you put fresh tomatoes or anything like that, it adds a little bit of color and some level of, let's say, "presentation." You just know it's going to have flavor in it. If you've never seen green mattar paneer before, it consists of green peas in a green stew-looking liquid, and you've also got clumps of cheese in there. Yeah, it's just as appetizing as it sounds. And it tastes awful, absolutely awful. Eliminating the tomato sauce drastically changed the taste, too.

One day, I got fed up and decided to test this whole red food theory. My brother, my sister, and I used to love those make-your-own-pizza-in-a-box things. We liked the Chef Boyardee brand. You make it and bake it at home. So, we made our own pizza and put the sauce on it, and everybody said to me, "Are you sure you want to risk this?"

"It's going to be okay," I replied. "Let's think positively. What's the worst that can happen?" So, we made the pizza, and I ate the SHIT outta it. Not even 30 minutes later, my right knee swelled up, and then both knees were swollen, and I was like, "Oh, my God, they were not kidding. I can't eat any red food!" Imagine that! HOLY SHIT they were right! Yeah, it goes without saying that I never rebelled like that again!

The next time I took homeopathic pellets, I followed the freaking instructions. Lol. This time, all I could eat while on the treatment was white foods: white bread, milk, apples without the skin, white rice, etc. I only took that medication once a week on Mondays, so all day every Monday, I could only eat white things. It was the weirdest thing, but I knew not to test any restrictive theories anymore because I'd already suffered immensely with the red food.

While I was doing all of these treatments, we ran into some family friends who told us that there was a Babaji (enlightened being) who was incredibly spiritual and holy, and He happened to be in Winnipeg, Canada, right now. "Why don't you take Rosy to go and see Him?" they suggested. "Maybe He can bless her, and she can be healed." My parents were desperate, and so was I. Nothing seemed to be working. And as much as I enjoyed consuming the homeopathic pellets and their restrictions, they weren't really helping me.

We called Him in Winnipeg and then decided to take a trip out there to see Him. We decided this because not only was He a very enlightened being, part of a well-respected family of Gurdwaras all over India, but my mom had had a miraculous experience with the same Gurdwaras when she was a little girl in India.

When my mom was nine, she lost her five-year-old brother. They were very close, so when he died suddenly, she was devastated and shut down. She started having fevers and wasn't eating well. This lasted for three years. So, my grandparents took her to see the Babaji at the time at the same Gurdwara. The Babaji that I would see was the "successor" to the one my mom saw. When they got in front of Babaji, my grandfather humbly requested a blessing for my mom. All Babaji did was raise His right hand. That's it. Then he sent them on their way. I don't know if it was hours, days, or what, but my mom basically had a miraculous recovery and turned back into the normal little kid that she had always been. She started eating again and had no more fevers. It was a true miracle.

That was what my parents wanted for me. Granted, my situation was considerably different than my mom's in that I was dealing with a *physical* disability rather than a mental shock, so I didn't know what to expect. My parents didn't know what to expect, either.

We packed up and went to Winnipeg, where we met with Babaji. While I did receive a blessing from Him, it wasn't the miraculous encounter we were anticipating. Still, I loved the overall energy and vibe I got from the Gurdwara. It was very peaceful, and I liked it there. I was super-pumped, thinking, *All right, this is a brand new journey.*

I had an enlightening conversation with a woman there who told me about vegetarianism. As you know, Sikhs don't eat meat, but my family does. She told me how it feels to be a vegetarian, that it's a very clean way of living, and that animals are living creatures, so you shouldn't consume them. But it was what she said next that made the most impact. She said, "When you eat meat, it's like having a graveyard in your stomach."

I thought, *Whoa. Hold up, sister.* That was a VERY graphic visualization for me and really hit home. It was weird. It was gross. It was scary and creepy. But it was all I needed to hear. I was convinced that I needed to stop eating meat. Not to mention, after we got back from that trip, I saw a *20/20* undercover report on the poor treatment of cows in slaughterhouses, and I was officially a vegetarian! LOL.

I decided to change my whole outlook on everything. I was the first person in my family to become a vegetarian. My mom followed, then my dad, and then my sister and brother. My siblings were shocked when I got home and told them about the change, but ultimately, everyone got on board, even my dad, who *loved* his three-minute eggs for breakfast!

After the trip to Canada, I was under the medical care of the Gurdwara and their doctors in India and around the world. I was getting some medications that were coming directly from India at this time. I tried Ayurvedic concoctions that tasted like dirt. I know that's an awful description, but it's the closest I can come to describing the taste. It was like muddy dirt and would make me gag. But it was supposed to help, so I kept taking it. I received special oils that were supposed to be massaged into my joints. Some caused more swelling and discomfort. It was very hit-or-miss. It was a very challenging time.

Life went on. I was a freshman in high school now, trying to live a normal life. There was one project that I did for my history class that I happened to be incredibly proud of. I made a reconstruction of the Battle of Little Bighorn on a wooden board. I was very creative, and I drew all the time, so this was right up my alley. Using a big piece of plywood for a base, I added little soldiers and Native American action figures to it, along with Play-Doh for terrain and glue with blue food coloring to make it look like a river running through it. I did a beautiful job and got an amazing grade on it. I wish I had a picture of it. I spent weeks designing and building it! Dearest reader, remember this project, okay? We'll circle back to it later in my story.

I took art in high school all four years. I loved art and the other classes that I took. The only downside was how much of a struggle it was to walk from class to class because the school was MASSIVE. My hands hurt when drawing, but I didn't want to stop doing it because I loved it so much. I was swollen A LOT, and I was hurting A LOT, so I stayed to myself a lot. I didn't really have any close friends in school because I wasn't able to do extracurricular things or go to school dances. To be honest with you, yeah, I wasn't allowed to do those things, but I also didn't have the energy to do them. Basically, when I got out of school, I went home and CRASHED. I'd sleep, and then I would get up and do whatever homework I had and whatever else needed to be done. I was getting up at the butt crack of dawn. Our high school started at 7:20 in the morning. That was the first class. Imagine having a chronic disease where you're swollen all the time and have a lot of morning stiffness. Getting up so early in the morning and trying to function is very challenging.

I was taking all these medications from India, along with Tylenol and Advil, all day long for pain management, and the combination of it all started making my stomach hurt like crazy. Our family doctor wasn't too impressed with Ayurvedic or homeopathic treatments. He told my parents, "You really should come back to the medical center and get her treatment done here."

Our response was, "No, we just don't believe in it. It ended up putting me in the hospital."

"Well," he said to me, "I'm actually going to be hospitalizing you anyway because it looks like you might have stomach ulcers." So, I got hospitalized for that, just for a day, so he could figure out what was happening with my stomach. He blamed it on some of the medications I was getting from India, which were aggravating my gut a little bit. Plus, I was also taking the highest doses of Tylenol and Advil. I'm pretty certain that it wasn't the medications I was getting from India that were creating the ulcers. It was the Tylenol and Advil that were destroying my stomach. I ended up having to take Pepcid daily for my stomach ulcers.

I went back to school again. As I mentioned, during middle school, I had a five-minute pass. I had it again in high school. I also got special help from my friends to carry my books and things for me because we didn't have backpacks back then. We only had lockers, and we actually used them. However, my locker was too far from all of my classes, and my hands and fingers couldn't lift the locker clasp to open it. Hell, I could barely twist the combination lock to the right numbers because of the pain and swelling in my fingers and wrist. Honestly, I didn't like asking for help. I didn't like drawing attention to my "disability." I didn't like people thinking I was different or weird.

My high school had an elevator, but there was only one, and it was next to the front office. So, if I was downstairs on the opposite side of the school from the front office and elevator, but my next class was directly above me upstairs, why would I walk all the way to the elevator, take it up, and then walk all the way back to get to my next class? That's A LOT of walking. I could not justify that much walking. It didn't make any sense to me. So, I chose to go up the stairs one step at a time, SUPER SLOWLY, and typically, on days with a lot of pain and swelling, I would cry the whole time. It was very challenging.

I already mentioned that I stopped riding the bus in junior high. I never rode the school bus at all during high school. My sister would drop me off on her way to college, and my mom would pick me up after school. The first ten years of this stupid diagnosis were an absolute nightmare, a complete struggle to function. I was a kid, but I felt like an old lady. It was just debilitating trying to get through school, trying to do all of my schoolwork, and making good grades. Believe it or not, I NEVER made less than a "B" in any class! Remember that. It'll come into play later in my story.

I would get home after school and sleep for hours. Simple daily tasks like walking, bathing, and writing became nearly insurmountable challenges. My fingers were so swollen that it was challenging just to hold a pencil, pen, or paintbrush, and my once lovely handwriting was now looking like "chicken scratch." I wrote very slowly. I drew very slowly. It sucked, and it still brings tears to my eyes today.

Clearly, I still have some traumatic issues about this time in my life, as it always brings me to tears. I was so young and confused and felt so incredibly alone. I didn't know why the fuck this was happening to me. Why do I have to suffer like this? Why are people telling me, "Damn, girl, what did you do? What did you do to deserve this?" And there I was, silently sobbing and dying inside. I didn't do anything. I didn't do anything. and when you say something like that to a child, it's absolutely devastating because, the whole time, you're thinking, *Shit, man, did I really do something to deserve this punishment? WHAT DID I DO TO DESERVE THIS?* It was too much.

Okay, so enough crying because I'm actually crying. I have to tell you a story about this one time. I don't even know who told my parents to do this. I'm telling you, when I say I have tried some crazy treatments and done some seriously crazy things to help me in my desperation, I'm not kidding. When you're desperate, you'll try anything to get better. You'll try ANYTHING to give you some sort of relief.

Someone told my parents that there was this person who was a healer, and he suggested that once a week, I should stay on the floor all day long. The entire day, from morning to night. Somehow, that would heal me. So, I started that ritual. I stayed on the floor. We chose Saturdays to do this because my parents could put me in front of the television, and I could watch Saturday morning cartoons. As long as I didn't miss *Muppet Babies, Punky Brewster,* or *Winnie the Pooh*, I was good! I would stay on the floor all day long. But obviously, my condition was such that I couldn't sit on just a floor. I could never sit on a hard floor. It was very painful for me to do that. I needed something with a cushion. So, my dad got my mattress out of the bedroom, just the top part of it, and put it down in front of the TV, and I would stay there all day long every Saturday for several weeks.

Needless to say, this did not cure me. My point in telling you this is that we took EVERYONE'S advice and were willing to do the most outrageous of things because, again, when you're desperate, you'll try ANYTHING! My poor parents just wanted me to be cured. It was gut-wrenching. I was the person suffering through it, and I guess it was easier that way. I can't imagine the feeling of helplessness when you have to watch your child suffer and struggle with something as horrific and debilitating as what I went through. It's horrible! I just can't even imagine how challenging that must have been for my parents.

I was also struggling with faith and religion, asking God, *"Are you really mad at me? Did I really do something wrong? Is there a way for me to fix this? I'm sorry! I'm so sorry. Please make it go away. I promise I'll be good."*

During this time, Babaji decided that they were going to build a Gurdwara here in Houston. We were going to Gurdwara more and more and trying to find peace in prayer and meditation. Services were happening daily in the early morning and evenings. We started going to more and more services, and we were exhausted. I was already fatigued because I had RA, but all of us were tired because we were busy all day long.

One day, on our way back home, we were two miles from the house. I remember this as if it were yesterday. My sister was driving, and I was in the passenger seat. My brother, two cousins, and my saji (my nanaji – mom's dad) were in the backseat. We didn't really wear seatbelts back then. It wasn't a law. My sister had her seatbelt on. I typically did not like wearing my seatbelt because it was challenging for me to get it on and off, but for some reason, that day, I put my seatbelt on.

There was a ditch on the right side of the road where we were traveling. My sister fell asleep behind the wheel, and our car went up a utility pole and flipped over. I remember seeing the pole, and then the next thing I knew, we were upside down in the ditch. I was screaming, and my sister was screaming. Both of us were suspended upside down because we had our belts on. Everybody else was in the back seat. No belts. I didn't see them in the back seat, and we only heard our screams.

The EMTs had to get the jaws of life to tear the car apart and get us all out of there. My sister, my two cousins, and I were sent to one hospital in an ambulance, and then they took my grandfather and my brother in another ambulance to a different hospital. And while we were in the ambulance, the EMTs asked us questions about our medical history, etc. We were all in shock. They asked, "Do you guys have any allergies?"

My sweet little cousin innocently said, "Well, I'm allergic to cats and dogs." My sister and I locked eyes and lost it. We snickered! It was so funny and random. LOL. It was *precisely* the kind of humor needed in this type of serious situation, and TO THIS DAY, that's one of my favorite random childhood memories because it truly helped relieve the tension from that traumatic event.

It was a massive accident, though. I had gotten glass in my hand from the broken windshield, and because we were taken to separate hospitals, we didn't know the extent of the trauma and injuries that my grandfather or brother had suffered. As I mentioned, my sister and I were in the front of the car, and my grandfather was in the middle of the backseat. He had my brother on one side and the two cousins on the other side. On impact, he'd thrown one arm over my brother and the other over my two cousins and taken the full impact of the crash with his chest. My brother was fine other than bruised ribs, but my sweet saji was paralyzed from the neck down. It was DEVASTATING!

We would go and visit him in the hospital. He was in the ICU for a total of – and I'm not even exaggerating this number because I read it in my dad's diaries – 123 days. When he got to the tail end of his hospital stay, they wanted to transfer him to a nursing home in Brenham because he'd been there too long, and Medicare would only cover so much. The day they were going to transfer him was the day he passed away.

That was very, very tough because, like I said, I had already lost my grandmother, his wife, but she had passed so peacefully. He would give meticulous speeches at Gurdwara, and he was such a scholar – so well-educated and well-spoken – and had the most absolutely perfect English. We loved him so much. He was wonderful, and his death was absolutely devastating, especially to see somebody so full of life in the ICU with tubes and machines everywhere.

We had the funeral, and the entire Sikh community showed up to pay their respects. That was one of the largest funeral processions I had ever seen. Cars upon cars upon cars, filled with people, all with their hazards on, came to pay their final respects to a pillar of the Houston Sikh community. My grandfather was very well-known and respected, and it was incredibly humbling to know how many people loved him, cared about him, and just respected him.

A year later, a distant family member came to visit us, and he questioned my parents' choices about my treatments and religion. He was just a really annoying person with bad energy. Thankfully, he was only with us for several hours, and then my dad had to drop him off at the airport. My dad took him to the airport in his beloved parrot-green Pontiac Sunbird. He LOVED that car. We all hated it because we thought it was ugly, but I think today it would be super cute! At the time, I thought it was too low to the ground, making it too hard for me to get in and out of, but my dad loved that little thing.

Anyway, my dad told us later that they got into an argument on the way to the airport. So, my dad was not in a good mood when he drove back home. He was stopped at a stoplight, and a drunk driver slammed into the back of his tiny little Pontiac Sunbird. Several hours went by, and we started to get worried. Our dad wasn't home from the airport by evening, and keep in mind that there were no cell phones at this time.

Finally, we got a phone call from Memorial Hermann Hospital informing us that Dad had been involved in a very serious car crash and had been life-flighted to the hospital. The only part of the car that survived was the front seat. That was it. Everything else was completely destroyed. The car was completely totaled. If you saw the damage, you would seriously wonder how the hell he survived that accident. First of all, that car was very tiny, and he was hit by a pickup truck. I don't think it was a big truck, but it was a pickup truck, nonetheless. We were told that the Sunbird was like an accordion, totally mashed in.

My dad had suffered a contusion to his head. What we didn't know at the time was that it would trigger seizures in him later. He was in the hospital for 17 days. That was very traumatic because we didn't know what was going to happen. It's bad enough to see your grandfather go through a daunting hospital stay for over 4 months in the ICU with a tracheotomy and tubes coming out of every part of his body, but it's even worse when it's your dad just a year later. This really tested my faith. First of all, I already had rheumatoid arthritis. Then my grandfather passed away, and now my dad had been in an accident.

Shortly after the accident, he had a seizure at home and fell off of the bed at 4 a.m. My sister heard the noise, and she ran into my parents' bedroom and saw him seizing on the floor. He bit his tongue so hard that he had a huge cut and ended up having to get stitches put in. We had to call 911 and everything. It was a whole deal. That is such a traumatic thing for children to go through, to have to call 911 on a parent. From that moment on, he had to take medications for anti-seizing to ensure that it never happened again.

By this point, we were all thinking, *What's going on with our family? Are we cursed? Like, what's happening right now?* It was so, so odd. We had to find solace wherever we could, and for me, that was music, drawing, and anything creative that I could do to escape from reality and float into a fantasy world.

But I wasn't doing very well. I was in bad shape for pretty much all of high school, but it wasn't until right before my senior year that I got to a point where I was having a very, very difficult time walking. Relapsing. Again. And it was like the same old thing over and over and over again and so frustrating. I missed the first day of school my senior year and then maybe went to school a few more days and then missed more school. It was bad. I was struggling. We had to talk to the counselors, and they said, "The only option we have for her is to go on something called 'homebound studies.'"

Homebound study is where a teacher brings classwork to a homebound student who cannot attend school physically due to extenuating health circumstances. I was still doing my schoolwork; I was just doing it at home. So, the teacher would bring me all of the assignments. She came twice a week and would give me the same assignments that my classmates were getting. And she would give me exams just as if I were sitting in a classroom. There were no open-book tests. I couldn't cheat because I was sitting at home. No, I had a teacher there monitoring me. That was such a depressing time. I missed my friends so much.

During the handful of days that I DID get to go to school, I met this wonderful girl in my art class. I loved the way she dressed, and she was uber-goth. She introduced me to Depeche Mode 2.0. My first encounter with Depeche Mode was the song "People Are People" when I was in middle school. She brought in a Depeche Mode cassette and started playing it. As I listened to the music, I was like, "Oh, my God, what is this delicious song? It is amazing. I love this."

"This is 'Strangelove' by Depeche Mode," she said.

"Shut up!" I said. "I love them! You know, whenever I drove back and forth to the hospital to get treatment, this band made me so happy!"

She made me a copy of that cassette, which was the maxi-single with a bunch of remixes of "Strangelove." I loved it and loved it. I mean, I would listen to it ALL the time. It was the BEST gift anyone could give me!

I was in homebound studies for the full first semester of my senior year. During that time, I found out that my friend had been killed in a hit-and-run. She died instantly. Someone had hit her and her friend while they were walking on the side of a busy road. When I found out about that, I lost it. She was such a good soul. I only knew her for such a brief moment, but the impact she had on me by making me a copy of the tape was huge. This girl had turned me on to Depeche Mode again, and now she was gone. It had gotten to a point where it seemed like life was just one depressing thing after another, but she reignited something in me that I needed because I felt like I was dying.

Immediately after this, I got some medication from India that I was told was really going to help me as a lot of people had found relief with it. This miracle homeopathic drug came to me in a powdered form that was dosed out into individual tiny pieces of paper that were then folded up into triangles. Every day, I would take one triangle and let the powder dissolve under my tongue.

I started that treatment in November 1988. All of a sudden, I started feeling amazing, and I thought, *Okay, they weren't kidding. This is somewhat of a miracle drug.* By January, the second semester of my senior year was about to start, and I was already feeling like a rockstar. I was even able to get on and off the floor by myself at Gurdwara! WHAT? Usually, my mom, my sister, or both would help me get on and off the floor whenever I went to church, and I hated it because everybody would stare at me. Now, though, I could do it by myself. It was great!

I went back to high school in person, finished my senior year strong, and graduated cum laude with honors! After all the health struggles I had, can you believe it? The ONLY downside was that the National Honor Society wouldn't let me be a member because I wasn't healthy enough to participate in any after-school activities. I was the ONLY student who graduated cum laude without the NHS stole. They were jerks! But I had my honors cords, and I was also a member of the National Art Honor Society.

"Broken Still Life" by Jasi Singh, displayed at the Museum of Fine Arts Houston during part of my senior year of high school.

I also had some badass drawings that I had done in my advanced art class that were displayed at some really cool places! One drawing was hanging up in the Hotel Sofitel in Houston for the celebration of the bicentennial of the French Revolution or something like that. And then, another one of my abstract drawings titled "Broken Still Life" was selected to hang at the Museum of Fine Arts for a month.

I was so excited and so happy. I decided, without telling my parents, that I was going to apply for college at the Art Institute of Houston because that's where I wanted to go to school. I also got admissions forms from the Parsons School of Design.

Art was my passion. It's what I wanted to study. I knew in the back of my head that they would never say yes to me going to the Art Institute of Houston. I just wanted to see if I could get in, so I went ahead and applied. I also applied to the University of Houston, and I got accepted to both schools. I knew I wasn't allowed to go to school for art, but that was okay. At least I'd gotten in, right?

I graduated from high school not just with honors but with medals! I got a medal in my accounting class and a medal in my business administration class. I also got an $800 scholarship from Delta Kappa Gamma business sorority. Man, I was on FIRE! There was no stopping me now! I seriously felt like I had my life back for the first time since my diagnosis in 1984!

It was 1989 now, and I was on top of the world, thinking, *This is amazing. Where has this medication been for five years?* I had a summer orientation at the University of Houston, and I decided that I would major in business since I had done so well in my business classes in high school. I got to stay overnight for the orientation! *WHAAAAAT?* It was like a sleepover! Something that I didn't get to do with my friends while growing up! This was the first time that I was out of my family home, feeling good for the first time in a really long time and actually experiencing what it would be like to be in a dorm and on my own.

Let me tell you, it was so liberating. I WAS FREE! LOL. It was so awesome! It was SO awesome, in fact, that I missed all of the critical portions of the orientation and had to pick my classes without meeting with an advisor… OMG. Guilty as charged. I WAS HAVING SOOOO MUCH FUN that I registered for three upper-level classes and three regular classes, so I would have a full load of 18 hours. I was going to take 18 HOURS in my freshman year. I was like, come on? If I can take seven classes in high school, why can't I take six classes in college? What's the difference? That was my thought process. I'm a badass and can do anything, right?

In high school, because of my health issues, I wasn't able to take driving lessons. So, my dad taught me how to drive. The summer after I graduated from high school, my dad started teaching me in June. I got my license in July. I practiced the route to the University of Houston only ONE time with my dad (ALL MAJOR FREEWAYS), and then I was set loose on my own. And if you have ever driven in Houston before, it's NUTS! I can't even imagine that I did it in a matter of months, and yeah, that kind of explains how horrible of a driver I am now. Lol. I did learn from my dad, so mad props to him for my driving lessons.

I started my first semester in college, and oh, my God, I had so much fun. For the first time in my life, I felt like I had control and that I could do whatever I wanted. However, my dad would track our mileage in the cars – not in a bad or controlling way, but more as a way of keeping the cars in check and making sure we were on top of oil changes, services, getting good gas mileage, etc. My dad would ask us to write our mileage when we got into the car and then when we got home. So, you know, I would fudge a couple of things here and there when I would go off and decide to have lunch or go to the mall with my friends. Or I would have study sessions scheduled with friends that just happened to coincide with lunch plans at the local Black Eyed Pea, where I'd have a bowl of broccoli cheese soup with their crack bread rolls and french fries. Oh, I miss that restaurant so much!

I had SOOO much fun, in fact, that it started to take a toll on my studies. Remember my grades in school? Long story short, never in my ENTIRE school life had I ever made a grade less than a B. NEVER. Even when it was a B, it was never a B-minus. It was always a B or a B-plus. NEVER had I EVER gotten less than a B in my ENTIRE LIFE. Stage set? Good.

Now let's zoom in on my face as I opened my... very... first... report card from my freshman year of college. I kid you not; I glanced at it and instantly shit my pants. I was like, OH MY GOD, my parents are going to kill me. I had not one, dear reader, not even two, but... FIVE C's and one B. FIIIIIIIIIIIVE! Not one measly A at all. And for those of you keeping count,

JASMINE SINGH

that's FIVE more bad grades than I had ever gotten in my ENTIRE SCHOOL
LIFE.

RSE	DESCRIPTIVE TITLE	CREDIT LEVEL	GRADE	GRADE POINTS
31	ACCOUNTING THEORY I	UN	C	6.00
73	INTRO TO COMPUT & MIS	UN	C	6.00
03	ENGL COMP I	UN	C+	6.99
01	THE U S TO 1877	UN	C-	5.01
13	FIN MATH WITH APPLS	UN	C+	6.99
00	INTRO TO PSYCHOLOGY	UN	B	9.00

*OMG, my parents are going to KILL me! At least 2 of the Cs were
a C+ though! Yeah, I tried that. It didn't work! Lol*

I was terrified to show that report card to my parents. You have to
understand that in Indian culture, you're held to a VERY high standard. Yes,
I know I had rheumatoid arthritis. Could I really get away with blaming it on
that? Nope. Not with the amount of fun I was having. Not to mention that I
was feeling like a rockstar for the first time in years! There was simply no good
excuse.

This was the best I had felt since being diagnosed by far. There was no
reason for me to have five C's and one B. I couldn't blame it on the disease
because it wasn't the disease's fault; it was mine because I was back to being
that pre-diagnosis person who was just having a good time, enjoying life,
hanging out with friends, and doing the things that I could not do when I was
in school. When this first semester of college started, I went buck wild. Now,
I wasn't doing anything wrong or, you know, REALLY bad. It wasn't that. I
was just enjoying my independence. Staying out of the house was really
important to me. I used to play outside all the time before I was diagnosed,
but I had been stuck inside for years. I MISSED THIS SO MUCH! I would go
to the study center or to Hermann Park and just sit there, either getting some
work done or hanging out with friends at the same time.

60

I also realized during that semester that I wasn't that keen on the business classes I was taking. I think I settled for a business degree to make my parents happy because I got a medal in high school for accounting and business administration. Granted, my grades in high school were impeccable. They were awesome. But it was high school and significantly easier than college. Once I started taking some of these accounting classes at the college level, I was like, man, there's no way. I do not want to do this for the rest of my life.

I snuck into an advisor appointment and changed my major. My dad was already not happy with the fact that my report card was hideous. My parents were *sooooooo* disappointed in me. The look on their faces when I showed them the report card was *awwwwwwwful*. I wanted to curl up in a corner and suck my thumb… It was that bad. But I knew a business degree was not what I wanted. I didn't know what to do. I just knew that I wasn't happy, and I wanted to do something that made me happy. I already had too much unhappiness in my life with this disease.

My dad found out that I had changed my major after he started seeing expenses for things like drafting equipment. He was not happy, telling me that if I changed my major, I would do so without his support. It was very sad. I was very sad. But I *really* wanted to do graphic design. I wanted to do animation, too, but they didn't have stuff like that back then as an actual major, so I couldn't choose that. I was going to combine classes in the technology department, where they were using AutoCAD and teaching the technical graphics part of it, and then my actual major on paper was graphic communications. That's what I wanted to do. Dad was not happy with it, so he decided that he was not going to pay for my education anymore.

Then I was like, *Okay, well, shoot. Now what am I going to do?* I didn't have a job, and we weren't raised like that. We were raised to live with our parents and stay there until we were on our own two feet, preferably after marriage. My parents were willing to help my siblings and me as much as they could so that we didn't have to work during high school. I wasn't able to do any type of work because of my health, so my brother, my sweet brother, helped me with my tuition, books, and supplies for the summer sessions.

I finished my spring semester very strong, and it was during that time that Depeche Mode released their album, *Violator*. *Oh, my God*, it was absolutely perfect timing. To this day, it is one of my favorite albums of ALL TIME!!!! Every single song is simply perfect. I listened to it in my car. It was the very first cassette that I purchased for myself. I had been saving up funds because cassettes were kind of expensive back then, I think maybe $12. I didn't have a job, but I would take a few dollars here and there from my dad's cash bag. The money was supposed to be for lunches and school stuff, but I saved it for music. Then Depeche Mode announced their Violator Tour, and I was determined to see them live!

I finished my second semester and decided that I was going to try to get a job over the summer while taking summer sessions at UH. We had some family friends who owned a chain of bridal stores, so I got a job working at one of their places, and I loved it! It was during that job that I met a young man whom I had a little crush on, and we started talking and became really good friends. I was very smitten with him, and he was very smitten with me. We talked all the time at work and on the phone.

Later that summer, in August, I went to the Depeche Mode concert. It was my very first concert. I went and got a ticket *by myself*. I didn't even care if anybody was going with me. One of my friends found out that I was going and decided to get a ticket in the lawn area. I was sitting in an actual seat, and I had paid for my ticket through a scalper because I was like, I don't care how much it costs. I want to go to this concert. Back then, tickets were $10–30 each. I paid $75 for my ticket because it was with a scalper. This band means everything to me. I even made my own shirt! I got a plain black long-sleeved shirt from Michael's, and I painted the red Violator Rose on it and wrote "DM" on the back. Everyone praised my shirt and asked me where I got it, and I told them I made it! I still have that shirt somewhere. I had the most amazing time of my life.

This is the shirt I made! A few years ago I was going to throw it away and decided to cut it up and keep it. I had NO IDEA that I would be writing my book someday!

My friend drove, and she sat on the lawn. I would get out of my seat every once in a while and go sit with her. It was my very first concert, and the energy was so incredibly magical. For two hours, my stress disappeared, my pain disappeared, and my diagnosis disappeared. I was living in the moment, surrounded by strangers who shared my passion for Depeche Mode. I didn't even realize how much music meant to me until I was in that environment with everybody around me who loved the band just as much as I did and knew all of the songs just as well as I did. It was amazing and perfect.

The band Nitzer Ebb opened for Depeche Mode that night, and they were another band that would become a favorite of mine, too. It was such a beautiful experience. The energy at that concert was simply magnificent and perfect! I wished that moment could last forever. What I didn't know at the time was that something was about to happen to me that would change the course of my *entire* life. At least I got to experience this concert first. I was grateful.

The concert was at the beginning of August 1990. The rest of that month was horrible for me, with pain and swelling. I started having a lot of pain in my knees; the swelling was coming back, and it was just horrible like it was at the beginning of the diagnosis. I thought, "What's going on? I'm still taking this miracle medication, so why am I hurting so bad?"

I'd started that medication in November 1988, and it was now the summer of 1990. We were going back and forth with the priests and doctors at the Gurdwara in India, trying to find out what was going on. "All of a sudden, Rosy's not feeling good," my parents told them. "She's getting way worse. She can barely walk. She can barely function. What is happening to her?" The doctors there started doing their own digging, and a few days later, they called us back and told us to immediately stop that medication. "WHAT?" we said.

"Don't ever take the medication again. Just stop taking it."

"Wait, what?"

"It was compromised. It was not natural at all. It was not homeopathic like we thought it was. It wasn't. It was actually steroids."

Silence.

Earlier in my story, I told you what steroids did to my legs and the incredible weight gain that I had in a short amount of time; that's what I was taking now. I also told you that steroids are something that you're not supposed to be on for more than a handful of months before you start gradually decreasing your dose. I had been taking these steroids from November 1988 all the way to August 1990! Twenty-two months! Almost two straight years. And who knows what dose I was taking? The damaging effects of steroids on your body and joints are horrific. With rheumatoid arthritis, your body starts attacking itself, primarily the cartilage, and steroids can eat up your cartilage, too.

That's essentially what had been happening. I'd been taking steroids for a prolonged amount of time without any type of blood work or supervision. I didn't have doctor's visits, you know what I mean? No one was checking my labs, my vitals, etc. I was getting everything from India, so I trusted that it was something good.

I want to pause and make this perfectly clear. I'm not saying that the Gurdwara was at fault here, either. Not at all! The doctor, whoever that doctor was, decided to pull a fast one. It's very disheartening, but bad people exist. Everywhere. And they take advantage of the less fortunate. It was awful because even the priests, when they told me about it, were very upset about the entire situation. They said, "We're looking into this right now. We're so sorry. Just stop taking it. Please don't take it anymore."

I had to detox from all of that crap to get it out of my system and started getting other Ayurvedic treatments to cleanse me. Sadly, the damage had already been done to my joints. I wouldn't realize how much damage was done until later, but it was bad. Pain, swelling, it was all back with a terrible vengeance, along with deteriorating joints this time. I was already struggling with religion, struggling to figure out why this was happening to me. I didn't want to live anymore. Basically, I had gotten to a point where I couldn't walk anymore.

I had just started my second year of college. I don't know how I drove there, but I parked my car and walked from building to building very slowly, with tears streaming down my face from the pain. My legs weren't straight. I didn't have a handicapped tag back then, which blows my mind. I wish I had looked into it and gotten one. It would have helped me, but I was so anti-disability back then, too. I didn't like people looking at me. Don't look at me. Don't call me disabled. Don't call me handicapped. There's nothing wrong with me. Nothing to see here. Keep it moving. I am a normal human being.

What the hell was I thinking? I was fighting for my life! I was fighting for some semblance of normalcy. I was like, quit treating me differently. I didn't want that. So, I didn't have a handicapped tag. I would get to my classes an hour early just so I could get a parking spot closest to the front because, by the time my day was over, I was too swollen to walk far. I would cry all the way from my last class, begging for it to be over as I walked back to my car.

It's so hard to explain what this relapse did to me. Essentially, my legs were closing up. It was like the tendons in the back of my knees were shortening, so I couldn't straighten my legs out all the way. I don't know if you've ever tried to walk when you can't straighten your legs. It's *very* challenging. You almost have to walk on your tiptoes. Try standing up from a seated position and taking a few steps WITHOUT straightening your legs all the way. It's fucking hard to do! And my knees were swollen, my ankles were swollen, my whole body was swollen.

I tried to figure out what the fuck was happening in my life. I would get to my car, turn the AC on, and wait until my panic attack subsided. Why is this happening to me? What is going on? What did I do? Did I do something wrong? The conversations I had with God during this time were intense. What did I do to deserve this? Why am I suffering like this?

I couldn't walk at all. First, I went one whole day without being able to walk. No school. Then I went two days without walking. No school. To put this into perspective, to go to the bathroom, my mom would have to put her arms underneath my arms, lift me from the bed, and very slowly drag me to the bathroom and sit me down gently on the toilet. I was hurting so bad that my dad had to install a soft toilet seat because the other one hurt my hips so much, and I used to throw myself down on the seat.

My dad also softened to the idea of my graphic design dream, and he bought me a drafting/art table that came with a rolling chair. One day, I thought, "Let me sit on that chair and try to roll myself to the bathroom." The house had carpeting, so it was challenging. Little did I know that I wouldn't be able to get out of that chair for a very long time. I would be confined to that chair for the next four years of my life.

CHAPTER 5

WHY IS GOD SAYING NOTHING?

NOTHING

Depeche Mode

This is one of my favorite Depeche Mode songs from
the Music for the Masses album.
Why do I feel like I'm a sitting target?
Sitting here praying when God is saying absolutely NOTHING at all?
What's the point of faith?

I had to withdraw from college, putting my education on hold for whatever this traumatic relapse was. These four years in a wheelchair, I cannot even begin to tell you how impactful they were in determining who I really am. The things I went through during this time were simply insane and sometimes unimaginable. Truly, the things a person will do, the lengths they will go to, and the sacrifices they will make for a cure or just for a second of relief are incredibly humbling. Until you live it, it's very challenging to understand. The overwhelming sense of loss. Not being able to walk, being completely dependent on my family for EVERY SINGLE TASK, unable to do anything for myself. I was at the mercy of everyone around me. While I was so incredibly grateful for their existence, love, and care, I felt sorry for them for having to care for me like that. I felt sorry for myself and our circumstances. I wanted it all to end.

I also found out who was in my inner circle during that time. When you're wheelchair-bound, you really do find out who your true soul tribe is. Not many friends stuck around for the long haul. Neither did family members. Don't get me wrong; it wasn't anyone's fault. We all have to live our lives. That is our purpose. For some crazy reason, my life was turned upside down, and I couldn't understand why.

We didn't have cell phones. Cable TV was around then, but we didn't have cable at my house. Remember, we were frugal. So, my entertainment was very limited. God, I wish I would have had Netflix or any type of streaming service back then. We didn't even have the World Wide Web back then! LOL! That's the "internet" for you young folks reading my book. I can't even imagine how cell phones or streaming would have changed my life back then. To be honest with you, I probably would have been even more depressed because then I would have seen a lot more of everybody else being normal while I was stuck in a wheelchair. *UGH.* That would have sucked more. So, never mind. I take that back. I had my boombox, though, and I had my music, and that's really all I needed.

I had a TON of treatments during the four years that I was in a wheelchair. It was absolutely exhausting, and it inadvertently turned me against Western medicine even more than what had happened to me the first time with steroids. If I had been monitored, maybe things could have been different. I don't know. It is what it is, right? Today, I'm the type of person who doesn't go back and revisit the past and do the whole "what if" scenario. But that's not who I was then. I thrived on the what-if scenarios to the point of mental exhaustion. Though I wasn't the spiritual person I am today, I still laughed, made jokes, made light of the situation, made my family happy, and overall tried to make the best out of the horrific situation that we were all in together. You have to find the positive to survive and try to deal with the cards that you've been dealt.

I spent a lot of my time researching treatments and remedies during the four years that I was in a wheelchair. Somebody told my parents to have a ring made for me with the purest pearl that they could find, without any imperfections in it, and set it in gold or silver – and it had to touch my skin. I like silver, so I chose silver. I still have that ring. I look at it sometimes

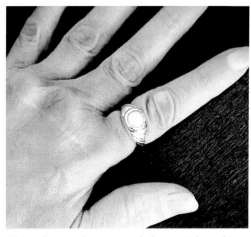

This is the ring that was made for me. I cleaned it up and started wearing it again.

and wonder if it did have some healing powers. Maybe I need to pull it back out again and revisit it. But anyway, we did have that ring made, and I wore it every freaking day.

I also spent six months in India with my mom. My poor mom, who is shorter than I am, had to push me around in a wheelchair. I packed all of my Depeche Mode cassettes and some other mix tapes, along with my Walkman, extra batteries, and sketchbooks, and headed to India with my mom. I can't even begin to tell you the type of struggle it was just to do the whole airport stuff. I had to use the wheelchair at the airport and then on the airplane. Remember, I was rolling around my house in that drafting chair for my art table because I refused to accept my "condition." I was stubborn. I didn't want it to be my reality. I was in serious denial.

I refused to accept the fact that I was wheelchair-bound, and I was determined to get out of the wheelchair. As far as I was concerned, it was unacceptable. I didn't want it. When we got to the airport, they put me in one of those super-narrow wheelchairs that can squeeze through the aisles. I had to cross my arms and legs so they could push me down the aisle. I don't know if you've ever seen a wheelchair-bound person getting loaded onto a plane, but that's how that happens.

First, we flew from Houston to Miami, and I threw up the entire way. I was so nauseous, and my poor mom had to handle me all by herself. I couldn't even go to the bathroom. Let me rephrase that: I *didn't* want to go to the bathroom because I knew what a struggle it would have been for my mom to handle me. So. I waited until we got to wherever we were going.

Next, we went from Miami to Frankfurt, Germany. It was the worst flight ever. I don't understand how a person with an empty stomach can still vomit. It was so bad. And when we landed in Germany, the plane stopped in the middle of the tarmac to deplane, which was so weird. I had never seen that before. I say this as if I'd flown a lot. Lol. This was only the third time in my life.

We landed on the tarmac, and everybody was just getting off the plane and going down the stairs, and I was like, "Uh, I'm in a wheelchair. I can't go down those stairs, so how is this going to work out?" Two massive, VERY German men – they were HUGE – walked toward me, and I thought, "Oh, shit, they're going to pick me up." Sure enough, they said something in German, and then they both lifted me right out of that seat, took me out of the plane and down the stairs, plopped me into a wheelchair, and rolled me into the airport. It was the funniest experience!

From there, we flew directly to India. Now, India is NOT accessible by the Americans with Disability Act (ADA). NOT EVEN CLOSE! So, I had to be carried everywhere. It was kind of a nightmare. Not "kind of a nightmare," it WAS a nightmare because I didn't know who these people were. Everybody was touching me and trying to get me up, and I was swollen and hurting, especially after being on multiple planes for 24 hours.

Finally, we arrived at our destination, and I got situated in the room where my mom and I would stay during our time in India at the Gurdwara. That was where the doctors who had been treating me after the steroid fiasco were coming to see me the next day. The good thing about my time in India was that I didn't have to travel anywhere, like to the doctors. They came to me. I just stayed in my room. At first, neither my mom nor I thought we would be there for too long, either. However, though the doctors promised to get me walking, they also said that they were not going to send me home until I was walking. Scary.

It was a lonely time. My mom and I bonded like crazy, though. It was during monsoon season, and it was always raining and super hot! They don't really have air conditioning in India – or what we know as air conditioning. I was sweating like a pig. It was very uncomfortable, but I was like, "Okay, let's give this a shot. We've tried everything we could back home. Surely, this can't be too different from that, right?" I was detoxing from all of the previous treatments I had tried and starting over from scratch. We're trying to get my health back in order!

For one of my major treatments, my mom had to purchase 22-karat gold bars that were melted down and injected into my thighs. The doctors built me a giant steam box out of wood with just my head sticking out of it. I would get into it through the side gate, and then they would put the hose in a bucket filled with super-hot water to create steam. I would sit in it for about 30 minutes to an hour.

There wasn't a whole lot to do since I couldn't travel anywhere, so I drew A LOT while I was there. I had my sketchbooks, my Walkman, and all of my Depeche Mode cassettes. During my short time in college and working at the mall, I was able to collect every single Depeche Mode album, along with a handful of singles tapes. Remember, I used to save all of the lunch money I took for college. Music was more important than eating. I loved shopping at Sam Goody, Hastings Records, and The Record Rack.

While in India, I went through batteries for my Walkman like nobody's business. The priests were *sooooo* very kind and generous; they would always go and get fresh batteries for me. They made me laugh, told me jokes, and kept me entertained. They were so incredibly kind to us. They ensured that my mom and I were very well taken care of. They were the first ones to introduce me to Chinese food! Noodles. In INDIA! Lol. I never had that before! They would bring me samosas and pakoras and totally hook us up with fun things! We were very blessed.

I was journaling a lot, too. I kept a diary of my time there and ran out of space several times and had to get more books to fill. There were beautiful peacocks right outside my door that I loved for like a whole day before I realized how awful they sounded! And I was like, "I swear to God, if these fucking peacocks keep screaming, I'm going to strangle them!" I was so annoyed at the peacocks that I found myself mocking them. Every time they screamed, I screamed the same way. My mom would crack up. It was how we kept ourselves entertained. Fast forward to the present day. Have you seen *Bridgerton* season two? If not, go watch episode six. They totally understood my annoyance with peacocks! Lol.

During these four years of being in a wheelchair, I started copping a major attitude! Hell, I was pissed. I started changing from the happy-go-lucky kid who'd found her life filled with trauma into an angry young adult. I got to a point where I was like, "I do not want to live like this. Why do I have to live like this? And who are all of these people who are visiting me in my room?" I felt like I was an exhibition, like in a museum or zoo!

It became known that there was this girl from America who was wheelchair-bound and staying in the Gurdwara, getting treatment done, and she was super-white (light-skinned, which is uncommon) and quite attractive, too – GASP – bechari. They were coming to me in droves, and they would touch me and say things like, "What did you do to deserve this? So sad, because you're so pretty. What a shame, what a loss." Most of the time, they were talking to my mom about me IN FRONT OF ME. My poor mom was right there, and she had to listen to it. I was just looking at some of these people in absolute awe and HORROR, like, *Do you not realize that I can hear you? I'm right here! There's nothing mentally wrong with me. Whatever you're saying to my mom about me, you're saying directly in front of me. I have rheumatoid arthritis. I'm not deaf, and I'm not dumb. I can understand everything that you're saying to my mother.*

Clearly, I had A LOT of anger about this back then. I have since healed from this trauma and chalked it down to pure ignorance. We all have to do better with the things we say to people who are suffering. Are my words going to help them or hinder them? It's very sad.

One memory in particular stands out the most. An elderly, well-respected man came to see me. The very first thing he said to me was, "I'm just coming back from the funeral of a girl who died of the same thing that you have, rheumatoid arthritis."

I was like, *DUUUUUUUUUUUDE, filter much?* I locked eyes with my mom; she locked eyes with me, and both of us were in complete shock. Like, are you serious right now? That's the first thing you say to us? That's the first thing that you choose to say when you walk into a room to a desperate mother and her disabled child who traveled all the way from America, struggling to get treatment while in a wheelchair? It was just unbelievable to me. I did end up forgiving him and letting it go because we saw him all the time, and he got better with his greetings.

We also made some really great friends there, too. I had an amazing aunt who lived in New Delhi and a niece and nephew who would visit me all the time. They brought me magazines. They would buy me snacks and special foods that I couldn't get at the Gurdwara because we had to eat whatever was being served at the church. So, it's not like I got any special foods or anything like that. They would bring fun snacks and things like that for me and basically just give me things to keep me busy and entertained. They brought me the best chips, orange Mirinda soda, and Namkeen. It was so good! And there was a moment when my mom and I decided to visit my dad's sister, who actually lived about three hours away, but the infrastructure is REALLY bad in India! It feels like six hours' worth of driving because the roads are so bad. You can't go so fast, and it's like *Ace Ventura, Pet Detective*, where you're bouncing up and down in the car. Remember that scene? We did that!

That's what traveling was like, and it was painful to do that. We visited with my aunt for about a week and then came back to Gurdwara in New Delhi.

Then we got transferred to one of the other Gurdwaras in a smaller village. A religious ceremony was going to occur, and they wanted me to experience it in person, so my mom and I boarded a van. I was carried in and then carried out when we arrived at the new Gurdwara. It was there that my mom and I opened up the back window in our room and took a whiff of the air. I was like, *Wait, what is that smell? That kind of smells like, dare I say, marijuana.* I asked the people there, "Is it really?"

"Yeah," they said. "It's kind of wild, and it grows back there."

I don't know if it affected me at all while I was there, but that was probably my first documented interaction with weed, which will come into my story later. But it just cracked me up that I was staying in such a religious, sacred setting and could smell the weed in the back. It was precisely the kind of comic relief I needed.

During this time, my dad, brother, and sister were back home. My mom got to talk on the phone with my dad and siblings every once in a while. I wasn't able to because the phone was too far away and I was confined to my room. My brother would record tapes for me, telling me all about his life and how much my dad, sister, and he were driving each other crazy! Lol. Meanwhile, my mom and I were starting to go crazy, too, and really getting on each other's nerves. We were on our FOURTH month in India, and I was seeing no improvement in my health.

My brother's recordings made me SO HAPPY! I loved them so much because I had not seen him in four months and his voice was changing. He was going through puberty. He was also talking differently because he'd started listening to a brand-new radio station in Houston called 97.9

One of the many drawings in my sketchbook from India

The Box, which was all rap. R&B and gangster rap were coming up at this time. OMG, y'all! It was so funny and awesome at the same time! My mom was so confused by his voice and what he was saying about the music he was listening to. It was quite an entertaining experience, to say the least! I couldn't wait to get back home and find out more! God, I missed my family so much. I would listen to his tapes on repeat. I would rotate between my brother and Depeche Mode while I drew and journaled. Being in a religious place, I listened to beautiful prayers and hymns every morning and late afternoon or early evening. All the other times, I had my headphones on while drawing, writing letters back home, journaling, and fantasizing about walking, dancing, and being normal again.

There are drawings that I did while I was in India and during the four years of being in a wheelchair that are absolutely my pride and joy. These drawings were very impactful. My hands were in such bad shape. It's a miracle I was even able to draw and write. They have so much meaning to me because they took so much time and effort for me to draw. My hands were slowly closing the same way that my legs were.

To help you understand the destruction of RA on your joints, open your hands in front of you (palms up). Now, gradually start closing them as if to make a fist. Right before your fingers start touching and right before you make them into a fist, that's how my hands were. I wasn't able to make them into a fist, nor was I able to open them all the way. It was HORRIFIC! That's how destroyed my joints were. All of my knuckles were so swollen, too, and my knees were practically at a 90-degree angle. When I slept, I had to have a pillow under my knees to keep them elevated. It's easier to lie on either side than it is to lie on your back without having some sort of support under your legs.

Being in India for so long was very challenging. We just didn't have the level of accommodations that we had at home. It was a huge struggle. Some people would get upset with us when we told them how much we missed home. They kept telling us to be patient. YOU try going through what we did. YOU try "walking" in my shoes. THEN talk to me. It had already been four months, and there was no improvement. I just wanted to go home. I wanted my own bed. I wanted my family. Remember the gold that they were injecting into me? I started getting gold specks in the whites of my eyes, and you could see it. That part was kind of cool.

But man, we saw *soooo* many things while we were in India. We saw people who were possessed. Yes, supernatural stuff is real. Spirits are real. One possessed person came up to our bedroom door, put his eye to the keyhole, and said in a very creepy voice, "Rosy, I can see you. What are you doing?" HOLY CRAP! I was just terrified! He would only do that when my mom left the room, and I was alone. Apparently, when you are in a place of religious worship and prayers, you can become compromised by evil spirits that are trying to keep you from praying and staying in meditation. I don't think I would have believed it had I not seen it with my own eyes. As far as I'm concerned, I saw it, I believe it, it's there, and I don't fuck with it. Keep your head down and keep moving. I often wondered if the Mary Jane growing in my back window could somehow have influenced me. Lol. Just kidding! Totally kidding!

Fast forward, and I was now in my SIXTH month of treatment in India. Funny story now; it wasn't funny then. We had flown on Pan Am, and if you know anything about Pan Am, well, they kind of went bankrupt while we were in India. So, by the time our trip came to an end and we were allowed to leave India, my dad had to buy brand-new tickets for us to fly back home, and he was not happy about that. Frugal. Lol.

I was so sad and so defeated in this picture.

I was sad because the treatments hadn't worked, and I was still in a wheelchair. My mom and I were both so defeated! If you look at the pictures we had taken for our Visas, you can see how much weight we both lost while there and how much older and defeated my mom looked. She was in her early 50s; that's how old I am now. It broke my heart.

The doctors had actually made me feel that I would be cured during my stay. "We are not going to send you home until you're walking. We're going to make sure we send you home walking." That's what they told my family back home. That's what they told me. So I was pumped. That's why I agreed to all of the treatments and did everything. My dream was to go home walking.

After six very long months, the same doctors who were once so hopeful and encouraging were now pretty much telling my parents, "Sorry, but there's absolutely nothing more we can do for her. You might as well take her home." That was it. It was over. Western medicine had failed me, and now, so had the Eastern side. It was HEARTBREAKING!

One day before leaving, there was a last-ditch effort made to have a healing bracelet made for me in this tiny village a few hours away. The priests had to carry me out of the van and into the healer's little hut and put me down on the ground in front of him. He did a little ritual, made the bracelet, put it on my wrist, and closed it up, and I was supposed to keep it on forever. I don't remember how long I actually kept it on, but I wore it for at least a few weeks. I don't even think I have that bracelet anymore.

Finally, my mom and I boarded British Airways and left India. One of the very first songs I heard on the plane was U2's "Mysterious Ways." It made me so happy. To this day, every time I hear that song, that's the first memory that pops into my head! And my sweet Depeche Mode? The amount of Depeche Mode I consumed while I was in India was unbelievable. I had every song memorized. I took solace in the songs. I honestly don't know what I would have done had I not had those cassettes with me. I don't know what would have happened to me while I was there. I don't know how I would have survived. I didn't want to be in a different country from my family while I was losing hope. When you start losing hope, that's really the most devastating, gut-wrenching feeling. When your doctors tell you that there's no hope, it's like, what the fuck am I supposed to do now? Western medicine had failed me, and now Eastern medicine was telling me there was nothing they could do for me. So, what the hell was I supposed to do? I was stuck. And I was only 21 years old. I turned 21 in India.

CHAPTER 6

WAITING FOR THE NIGHT TO FALL

WAITING FOR THE NIGHT TO FALL
Depeche Mode

This beautiful song became my nightly mantra.
I wanted it all to end.
I wanted the night to fall.
To save me from this awful reality.
Only at night did my life become bearable, and I felt tranquility.

W hen we got home, I was not doing well health-wise, but I was SO HAPPY to be back home! Life continued as "normal," my new normal. I was still in a wheelchair, still trying to find solace in music and drawing, but I became a hermit. I NEVER left the house. Remember, I did NOT accept my circumstances. I REFUSED to accept that this was truly my life. We returned from India in January 1992. From 1992 to 1993, I had more random treatments, was still in a wheelchair, still at home, and DID NOT LEAVE MY HOUSE. I was scooting around my house in an office chair. I had lost something crucial during this time: hope. I had no hope of recovering. All doctors seemed to have given up on me, and there didn't seem to be any hope of me walking again. I was depressed.

At this point, two of my high school friends found an "abandoned" wheelchair in their apartment complex and brought it over for me. At least, that's what they told me, lol. I fear they stole it, but let's try to stay positive and say that it was abandoned. It was a hideous brown color and had hospital lingo written on the back. So, being the creative person that I am, I got out my Sharpies and went to town decorating my wheelchair. I wish I had a picture of the design I drew on the back. It was pretty cool looking. And having it allowed me to get out of the house every once in a while. To be clear, I was NOT able to roll myself around in it because my arms, wrists, and hands were in horrible shape. I'm not sure if I mentioned this, but most of the time, I needed help getting on and off couches, chairs, beds, toilets, etc. I was completely dependent. You don't even want to know what we had to do in India because there was NO rolling chair in our room. I had to be moved from stool to stool to stool to stool to make my way to the bathroom. Every single time. It was bad.

Music came to my rescue again, and I got a brand-new boombox in my bedroom. I was already liking the gangster rap that my brother was listening to, but another genre was entering my life around this time. I'd always liked dance music, but I was really getting into techno/trance/club music. I noticed that our local radio stations were starting to go live and broadcast live from different clubs around town. The music they played during the live broadcasts from one of these clubs was very different from the pop music that they played during the day on the radio! It was stuff I had NEVER heard before, and I LOVED it! I was like, what is this music?

It was underground dance music/alternative dance music/industrial dance music. It was very different from anything else I had ever heard before. There was one particular broadcast on 93Q. They would play live from a club called Detour. OMG. Talk about a game-changer! To this day, I still have around ten cassettes that I mixed myself on my boombox from recorded tapes! It was every Saturday night, and it gave me something to look forward to! For the first time in YEARS, I felt like I had a purpose! Yes, I know how incredibly sad that sounds. Here's this disabled 21-year-old in a wheelchair with zero hope of walking again, looking forward to a live radio broadcast so she can put her headphones on, close her eyes, and pretend she's there, walking, dancing, and being normal.

Every Saturday night, from 10 p.m. all the way to 2 a.m., I would listen to this live broadcast and record it. Then I found out that one of the DJs who was doing the live broadcasts also worked at a record store in Houston. I would call the record store, and we became friends over the phone. After each broadcast, I'd ask him if he could tell me the names of the songs and artists he'd played the previous night. I would play a little snippet of the song, and he'd give me the info. He didn't have to do that. He could have blown me off and told me to get lost. Maybe he felt sorry for me? I don't know. I didn't care! We bonded with music!

He was so sweet and accommodating, letting me ask him anything I wanted about the cassettes that I had recorded. I was such a loyal listener. I did this week after week after week. Everyone in the DJ booth and at the record store knew me and my story, and they knew that I was wheelchair-bound. That's why I couldn't go to the club. But I listened every Saturday night. Sadly, the club was permanently shut down before I ever had a chance to go. It was so sad. I was losing the one thing that I looked forward to the most.

I got to listen to it for about four months before the final broadcast. It was a two-night spectacular event, Friday AND Saturday night, live from Detour. On night two, The DJs decided to do something special for me during their final live broadcast. They gave a shoutout to me and played my favorite song from the Detour broadcasts called "Crack Train" by Midi Rain.

You're not going to believe this, but the BEST part of this story is that I *never* got to actually hear the shout-out live that night. Let me explain. I was so incredibly sad that it was the final night of the broadcast that I stopped my recording early and went to bed! I found out the following day when I spoke on the phone with my DJ buddy. He asked me if I had heard the shout-out. I had to pretend that I heard it! It was so touching!

And here's where the story gets EVEN BETTER. Fast forward to 2019. I was downloading some old DJ sets, and I found a site that houses old live radio broadcasts. Y'ALL!!! DETOUR WAS ON THERE! Not all of the broadcasts, but the final broadcasts! *WHAAAAAAAAAAT?* Scan the QR code below to experience it yourself.

Detour Live on 93Q – The Final Gathering (April 13, 1991).
Fast forward to about 02:01:20, and you'll hear it!

Twenty-eight years after the original broadcast, I FINALLY got to hear it for myself! I got to hear them do the whole shout out to me. They said, "Jazzy, this one's for you!" while playing my favorite song in the background. OMG! I cried like a baby! It was even more magical than it would have been that night in 1991!

I was so incredibly sad when the broadcasts ended, but at least I had my cassettes. I was so grateful that I had those recordings, and I listened to them nonstop. It was so beautiful to finally get to listen to that final night after such a long time. I don't think I mentioned this yet: My best friend in seventh and eighth grade gave me the nickname Jazzy, and it stuck!

This is my Detour collection. I made all of the covers using magazines and paint markers and I wrote all of the artists/song titles inside.

Anyway, back to the story. After the Detour broadcast ended, someone told my parents to take me to a homeopathic doctor in Houston who they had heard was pretty good. Buckle in tight; this story is a doozy! I will not say his name, but I have given him a very bad review on Yelp, Google, and everything else simply because of my experiences there. Let me preface this by saying that I totally believe in homeopathic treatments; it's just that my situation seemed to be something very unique that could not ever be "cured."

Keep in mind, the very first thing doctors in the medical center told my parents and me was that there is not now, nor will there ever be, a cure for juvenile rheumatoid arthritis. So, it was hopeless anyway, right? Plus, there was something clearly wrong with my joints. I just didn't know the extent of the damage at the time. And honestly, no one, not even our family doctor, bothered to X-ray my joints. Isn't that crazy? NO ONE! We didn't even think about it!

Anyway, this guy had me sign all sorts of forms and NDA-type stuff in the beginning, saying that I wasn't an undercover agent. That was a huge red flag, but when you're desperate, you'll try anything. And keep in mind that insurance didn't cover alternative treatments back then. So, insurance wasn't going to cover any of this. My parents were paying cash for this.

So, we went to see this doctor, and he put me on seaweed and pellets that I had never tried before. None of those worked for me. And, yes, I'm well aware that you have to give natural treatments time to work, but I was 21 years old and confined to a wheelchair. I had nothing to lose. I needed shit to work. I needed my life back and not broken promises.

He did allergy testing on me and got me on an allergy shot that he would give me through a drive-thru type thing. We would drive up, and because I was in a wheelchair, I didn't have to get out of the car or anything. They just came to my side of the window and gave me my allergy shot, and I went on my merry way. Then, he got this new breakthrough treatment called bee venom therapy (BVT or apitherapy). They are injections filled with bee venom and are highly potent. I had to bring an ice chest with ice packs with me to every appointment, along with an EpiPen® in case I had a reaction.

I began with a couple of injections at a time, which eventually became a consistent 20 injections at one time. Yes, you heard that right: 20. TWO ZERO. You could either get those injections in your legs, your arms, or along your spine. I chose to get them in my arms and my back because it would have been too uncomfortable and painful in my legs. That's 20 bee sting injections at one time. If you've *never* been stung by a bee before, it's incredibly painful. And if you *have* been stung by a bee before, take that single bee sting and multiply it by 20. That's what I would get down my arms and back. One week, it was down my back; the next week, it was down my arms. They just rotated the injection sites.

After treatment, I would get situated in the car with an ice pack on my back. I remember leaning back into the seat, and the ice pack felt so cold but so good because my entire back was on fire. I felt like I was on fire. I would look out of the car window on the drive home with tears streaming down my face. I didn't want this life. I didn't deserve this kind of pain. I wanted to end it all. I fantasized about opening my car door while we were on the highway and launching myself out. But I didn't want to be left in the hospital in a vegetative state. Especially after seeing my grandfather in the ICU. I wanted it to be over, and there was no guarantee that I wouldn't make my situation worse.

I thank God my dad was keeping diaries and journals during this time, and I'm glad I read them before writing this book because I found out after reading his journals exactly how many injections I had gotten. In total, and I'm not exaggerating, it was 333 bee sting injections! They cost my parents $7.50 a pop. After the 333rd injection, I went into my next appointment with him and asked why I hadn't seen ANY improvement when I'd been on this treatment for about 16 weeks already and had had hundreds of shots. When was I supposed to see results?

He said that I had to be patient and that it would take about three hundred or so injections before I started feeling any kind of a difference or change. I was like, *Why the hell didn't you tell us that before we started this? I would NOT have agreed to three hundred BEE STINGS! WTF, man?* I was LIVID! I was so mad at him and his whole practice and what he said. How DARE he! Please don't misunderstand; it's not that I didn't think the therapy was viable. I'm sure it IS! I was angry because he didn't tell us that, and my poor parents had to pay cash. All of these medical expenses were becoming too much.

Then he started doing this kinesiology thing where they tested my vitamin and mineral deficiencies based on how easy it was for them to pull on my arm. Basically, you lie down with your arms flat on your sides, bend your right arm at the elbow, and hold it tight or flex when they repeat a mineral name. Apparently, if you don't hold your arm taught enough, and it's too easy to push down, you're deficient in that mineral. Yeah, I didn't feel like this was legit, you know? I caught on, though, and started flexing harder. I figured *If I hold my arm as tight as I can, they can't pull it down. That means I'm not deficient in that vitamin/mineral.*

It was *SOOOOOOO* gut-wrenching. I felt so betrayed. I couldn't seem to catch a break with doctors. One disappointment after another. I felt so defeated, so used, so manipulated, and so disappointed. I said, "That's it. I'm

DONE!" And I leaped off of the examination table and into my wheelchair and rolled my ass out of there. Did that hurt? Yes, it did. I believe I mentioned this already, but I couldn't roll myself because of the condition of my hands. But I did it that day! Adrenaline rush!

Both of my parents were in the waiting room, and they said, "Hey, what's going on? I thought you had your appointment."

I was like, "Nope, we're done. And we're never coming back here again. I'll explain everything in the car." I told them all about it in the car, through raging tears, and said, "I'm just not doing it anymore. I'm sick and tired of this bullshit. This is ridiculous." Thankfully, my parents supported my decision and completely agreed. Another failed treatment option.

My dad was seeing a chiropractor around this time, so he decided to take me to see if there was any promise in that kind of treatment. Yes, I know, many of you are SCREAMING, "NOOOOOOOO! You have RA! Don't do it!" Well, I didn't know that at the time. So, yeah, there's that.

The chiropractor treated me by doing spine and neck adjustments, which, surprisingly enough, did not hurt me. I also got physical therapy, heat therapy, and massages. He was cracking me and stuff but very gently. It wasn't like it was a cure or anything, but I wasn't in excruciating pain anymore. The swelling was still there, and the damage had already been done to my knees, so it wasn't like I was going to walk again with chiropractic care. At one point, he mentioned that I should look into total knee replacement surgery. That scared the shit out of me! But I started researching it at the library.

I started feeling more depressed in terms of trying to figure out why all of this had happened to me. I started digging into astrology, digging into my sign, digging into numerology, tarot, the I Ching, tea leaves, dream analysis; the list goes on and on. I was looking into so many different things, trying to figure out if I could somehow find the formula that would at least get me out of this damn wheelchair. I tried so many different things.

I even tried a nutritional supplement that my co-worker at the mall got me into. You know, the job that I only got to work at for like three months or so before I had my massive relapse and ended up in a wheelchair? She had started this powdered supplement, and she convinced me to start taking it, too. I started taking it and felt pretty good, so I became a distributor. Then I got my family members involved, and they became distributors, too! Lol.

Yes, I know it was a pyramid scheme. I know that now. And yes, it was just like Mary Kay. And yes, I actually DID sell Mary Kay for a hot minute right before my relapse, too. I had to send all my shit back to Dallas because I couldn't do it anymore because I was in a wheelchair. It was a mess! So, I became a distributor, and part of my responsibilities was to attend their meetings that were held at various hotel ballrooms. Because my family members were distributors, some of my younger cousins got to go to the meetings with me. OMG. We were so excited to get out of our homes. We used to go to these meetings, and we would fit SIX of us in a tiny little four-seater Toyota. These girls came to my house, all huddled in the car. They got me in and put my wheelchair in the trunk.

I kid you not; some of us were sitting on top of each other or on the floor. Not me, of course. Because I was in a wheelchair, so I always had a seat, as did the driver. But it was a free-for-all for the rest of the cousins! Somebody was sitting on the floor in front of me with no seatbelts; we didn't give a shit. It was so funny. Yes, I know it was dangerous, but we were kids. Well, okay, so I was kind of an adult, but I kind of wasn't. I was as naive as they come! I'd been sheltered for YEARS!

We went to these meetings with six of us packed as tight as sardines into a Toyota Corolla. It was so much fun. We would jam out to my Detour cassettes and club mix tapes. By this time, I was mixing my own cassettes and making tapes for my family, too. My inner DJ was THRIVING!!! I was DJ JAZZY! After Detour shut down, I started getting into hardcore dance/rave music. It was intense!

These are some of the cassette covers that I drew by hand.

My brother would take me to the library, and that's where I would do research on knee replacements and different arthritis treatments and such. I was also getting into historical romance novels. I was like, *All right, if I'm never going to get married, I might as well read about other people having a good time.* I found an author named LaVyrle Spencer and read all of her books… ALL of her books. There was one book in particular called *The Gamble* that I absolutely loved. I loved it so much because it's about a woman named Agatha who has a disability. She overcomes her challenges and falls in love with a man who loves her just the way she is, disability and all. It was so endearing. But it was also just a book. Shit like that doesn't happen in real life, right? I really just saw myself in that character and was like, *Oh, if that can happen to her, surely, it could happen to me.* Lol. Maybe somebody out there would love me, too. I mean, I was not Quasimodo or anything, but that's how people made me feel sometimes. Having a disability is such a stigma in society. And that's so sad.

Then the Super Nintendo came out, and IT CHANGED MY LIFE FOREVER! My brother convinced my dad to get it and to get us a small TV that we could leave in my room. Video games became a brand-new, wonderful escape from reality. We played EVERYTHING! We had all of the Mario games; Super Mario Bros. 2 was my favorite, and I could play it all the way through without dying if I played as Princess Peach. The catch was that I could only play for a little while at a time because of my hands. UGH. It was so frustrating. We played so much Street Fighter and Mortal Kombat. Then we got Super Mario World. And Metroid Prime! We would spend HOURS playing that game, along with Legend of Zelda: A Link to the Past. I have that Zelda game and that Metroid game memorized… I know where all of the super missiles are, regular missiles, the bombs! I had so much fun doing those things. It was very difficult for me, though, because I couldn't hold a controller for too long without my hands getting all messed up and my thumbs getting swollen, so I would play for a little bit and then hand the controller over to my brother and then just watch him play. And I loved it. It was so much fun. It made me so incredibly happy. We would play music in the background and enjoy playing video games all night.

My brother loved playing basketball outside, but he was hitting the ball up against the top of the garage and messing up the paint. So, my grandfather decided to make him a basketball goal out of wood. I know, so sweet, right? He surprised my brother with the goal one day, and we all went outside to check it out. It was so cool! He'd done a great job making it by hand. It was weird, though. It looked somewhat familiar to me. Like, where did he get the wood from?

Remember that beautiful history project that I did in high school that artistically displayed the Battle of Little Bighorn? The one that I created with my jacked-up arthritic hands? Yeah, that one. My brother asked Pitaji (what we called my paternal grandfather) how he made it. In Punjabi, he very nonchalantly told all of us that he found some wood with a bunch of crap all over it. He removed everything and refinished it to be a backboard for a basketball goal. Y'ALL! Remember my award-winning, super-creative high school history project where I reconstructed the entire Battle of Little Big Horn? IT WAS NOW HANGING ON THE TOP OF OUR GARAGE!

Now, as amused as I am about this story today and how we laugh like hyenas whenever we share the story with others, it was NOT funny then. I was in a wheelchair. I was angry. My life sucked. And now my project was gone? Do y'all even KNOW how much of a struggle it was to CREATE this thing? And now it was gone? COME ON!

I can laugh at it now because I'm healed, but then I was sooooooo pissed. But I had to give it to Pitaji because he was so incredibly skilled at carpentry work, and bless his heart, he made up for it by making me parallel bars from scratch! Who does that? Pitaji, that's who! He got the bars, and he sanded them down so I wouldn't get splinters and stuff in my hands. He said, "Rosy, we are going to get you out of this wheelchair, betta (an endearing Punjabi term for sweet child). We are going to get you up. We're going to get you walking." His solution was to make parallel bars so I could just stand up and start walking. I tried to explain to him that that was not the issue. He didn't get it. LOL. Anyway, The issue is I don't have any cartilage in my joints. It was too hard to explain. He just didn't understand it. But it was the thought that counts, and it was such a sweet gesture.

The parallel bars were massive and only fit in the living room. That's where I would appease him by trying to walk. I could hold onto the bars and kind of suspend myself there for a bit, but there was no walking happening. Clearly, there was something wrong with my knees. I would play music on our sound system in the living room while I attempted to "walk" with the parallel bars. The music motivated me so much! At this time, I had a cassette with Snap!'s "Rhythm Is a Dancer" and Haddaway's "What Is Love." It absolutely THRILLED me when my parents expressed an interest in both of those songs, and my dad used to request that I play them! It was so cute!

One time, I was home with only my grandparents, and I fell out of my little drafting chair that I was scooting around the house in. I fell! Did I mention that we had carpeting in our house? It is REALLY difficult to scoot around in a cheaply made drafting chair with small plastic wheels ON CARPET! The carpet in our house was bubbling up, and my family had to clean the wheels of the chair every so often because they would be filled with hair from the carpet! It was like a vacuum, but not.

So, I fell off of the chair because I rolled over one of those carpet bumps, and I started laughing because that's what I do. When I fall, or other people fall, I laugh because I think it's hilarious. The moment I fell, my sweet grandparents rushed to my rescue. They thought I was crying. This triggered my hysterical laughter. OMG. It was SO FUNNY! And I was like, "I'm not crying. I'm not crying." And they were like, "Oh, my God. Oh, my God. Oh, my God."

As they struggled to get me off the floor, I was cracking up because, one, I fell and, two, these two elderly people were trying to lift me off the ground, AND they were NOT going to be able to do it because the laughing was weighing me down so much. It just made the situation and circumstances even funnier, and I couldn't stop laughing. It wasn't until a little while later that they realized that I wasn't crying but laughing. Then they started laughing with me. I was never one to take things too seriously, and falling out of my chair in such a vulnerable state was utterly hilarious to me. Sad? Perhaps, but funny, nonetheless.

Have you ever been to a psychic? There's a super famous one in Houston named Cau Chin. I think he's still around to this day. He doesn't take appointments or anything, and it's first come, first serve. People stand in line for hours to see him and get a reading. There's a tiny waiting room inside, but it's usually full. Some people have to wait outside of his facility. We went there two times, once while I was in a wheelchair and once right after I got out.

The process is interesting. He speaks very little English and talks VERY fast, so you have to listen very closely. You sit down in front of him, and he just starts speaking. He goes year by year and shares visions of what he sees happening for you. He tells you the year you're going to get married, the year you're going to have a kid, the year you're going to have a successful career, the year you're going to have difficulties, and he just goes on and on. He talks so fast that you have to tape-record it, and then they give you the recording. You have an opportunity at the end to ask a few questions. It was just a crazy experience. I took notes after listening to the tape recording both times. There was nothing that he said that actually happened when he said it would. I think I lost ten years of my life from the first time I saw him to the next. Lol. It's cool.

Do I believe he's the real deal? For some people, he really is. I just thought it was kind of interesting and funny to a certain extent because, again, you'll do anything to find relief, find a solution, find help, find guidance, get knowledge, and just figure out how to make things better, how to have an actual life. HOPE. Any hope, even if it never happens, is still HOPE. He said I would get married, he said I would have kids, and he said I'd be successful. Who knows!

CHAPTER 7

AM I GOING BACKWARDS?

GOING BACKWARDS
Depeche Mode

Why do I feel like I'm going backwards?
Why does it feel like the misery keeps piling on?
I literally have NOTHING left inside of me.
I FEEL nothing anymore.
I've lost my soul.

It was now January 1994. Remember how I mentioned that I met a nice young man whom I kind of had a crush on when I worked briefly at the mall at a formal dress shop? We were talking the entire time I was in a wheelchair, and my parents even allowed him to visit me at home a few times. Well, he called me on the home phone one night because, you know, that's how we had conversations back then. I remember that night vaguely. I was sitting on the recliner, watching the Winter Olympics, and he called and asked me, "You walking yet?"

"Nope, still in a wheelchair."

"Hey, so I've met somebody, and I'm getting married."

Silence.

I was like, "Oh, okay, because I thought we were going to try to get together after I started walking again." Granted, I understood my circumstances. I was in a wheelchair, not walking. What was the hope here? What would happen? Nothing would happen. When he told me this, I was devastated. I went into a VERY major depression. I started getting cystic acne on my face, and things seemed so devastatingly hopeless.

My friends had acquired a decent wheelchair for me, but it was in very bad shape. So, my family and I decided to go to our family doctor to get a prescription for a REAL wheelchair because I'd finally caved and "accepted" my circumstances. I had lost all hope. I had no idea what I needed to do to get a wheelchair. I needed to be able to get around and actually LEAVE the house. By this time, it had been over three years since I'd last walked. Remember, I'd rarely left my house since the relapse. Well, I did for the India trip, but even then, I never left the rooms I was in. Basically, I shut myself away from the world and became a major recluse.

When my doctor entered the room and saw me, he said something pivotal that was *precisely* the "fire" that I needed to make a change in my life. While giving me cortisone shots in my knees – they were in REALLY bad shape and so painful – he said he'd gladly write me a script to get any wheelchair I wanted, but he *highly* recommended that I just deal with my situation, accept my circumstances, and get an electric wheelchair. He basically told me to toughen up and just get used to it. He told me to go back to college and move on with my life… in an electric wheelchair.

His words absolutely destroyed me. I'd gone in there thinking, *Okay, fine, I'll get a wheelchair. Let's do this. Let's do this recovery.* But when he said "electric wheelchair," that turned it into a permanent disability versus a temporary thing. And don't get me wrong, I KNOW it had been three years, and there didn't seem to be ANY HOPE at all that I would ever walk again. I just didn't want to hear it. It was so pitiful.

I was so angry that I NEVER wanted to see him again and didn't ever want to be treated by him ever again. I left there very upset, but he did give me one piece of advice that would end up being very beneficial, which is why I forgave him. He suggested that I apply for disability and get on Medicaid because I was 23 years old, completely dependent on my parents, and didn't have any type of insurance or anything. He also mentioned that there were some promising treatments for JRA that had not been available ten years before, and I might find something that would work for me.

So, I decided to go ahead and apply for disability and Medicaid. To qualify for disability, I had to be evaluated by a doctor. In my case, that was an orthopedic surgeon. As I was going to this appointment with my parents, I had just purchased the brand new Culture Beat CD. Remember the song "Mr. Vain?" I had that album cranked up in the car, driving my parents crazy. I knew my parents weren't fans of me listening to so much music, but it HEALED me. It soothed my soul, and quite frankly, it was ALL that I had. When I put music on, on my boombox or with headphones, I was able to escape my horrible reality and transport myself to a magical world where I was dancing, walking, and living independently without any limitations or disability. It was simply perfect. If I hadn't had access to music, I don't think I would have made it. And keep in mind, now that I had been back from India for a couple of years, my brother had introduced me to gangster rap. This was PHENOMENAL! I took to that genre of music SO QUICKLY because it allowed me to express all of the pent-up rage inside of me.

And the dance music! I LOVED dance music in general, but this new techno craze, BPM, EDM, house, ambient, drum and bass, I was IN LOVE!!! And Depeche Mode started getting in on the action with the single remix tapes. They always had dance remixes to most of their popular songs, but this was taking it to the NEXT level of awesomeness! I started getting more into dance music and just listening to everything. There were live broadcasts of local raves on Rice University radio, and I would stay up and record some of them. I have over 30 of those recordings!

*My Rave collection! I made the ones on the left. The ones on the right
are from raves and from Mr. Yuck!*

Thank God I had music to keep me sane because I was so angry during
this time. I was angry at the doctor. I was angry at my circumstances. I was
angry that I was applying for disability even though I was only 23 years old. I
was like, *What kind of life is this? Who wants to live like this?* This was
definitely the birth of OG Jasmine. Lol. I was MAD. I was like, *Fuck this shit!
I am done with this! You want to deal me these cards? Okay, then I'm going to
make the best of this situation! There has to be a better way, and DAMN
STRAIGHT, I'm going to find it.*

Disability sent me to an orthopedic surgeon to get evaluated to find out
exactly how disabled I was. That might sound like a joke, but it's not. How
disabled are you? I'm so disabled that... Okay, that's enough. Anyway, I went
to this appointment, and he took X-rays of me. This was the first time my
joints had been X-rayed since my diagnosis in 1984, ten years before. He
examined my hands, which were practically closed. My feet, too, were in very
bad shape, and my knees were stuck at 90-degree angles.

He asked, "How the hell did this happen?" and we gave him the long-
story-short type deal. The X-rays showed massive destruction. I had ZERO
cartilage left in my knees, right ankle, most of my toes, both wrists, and all
finger joints (especially the MCP joints). Basically, It was bone on bone. The

cartilage was SO destroyed that there was no visible barrier between my joints in the images. Some joints seemed to blend into one another. There was simply no cartilage left. My knuckles, no cartilage left. My wrists, no cartilage left. He didn't do my elbows. He didn't do my shoulders. He did my feet. My toes didn't have any cartilage. It was just massive destruction everywhere.

He said, "If you don't get approved for disability, I don't know who will." So, he signed off on my disability, and I decided I trusted him and wanted him to be my doctor. First, he put me on different medications. He said, "There are a lot more treatments now than there were before you started this journey ten years ago. There have been some big advances made in arthritis research."

I started taking some medications that helped me with the pain and inflammation. He also started me on physical therapy. This was the first time in years I was getting some sort of relief! But at the end of the day, my cartilage was already gone, so the joints were destroyed. The only hope I had for actually walking was to have my knees replaced. The problem was, I was 23 years old, and my doctor told me, "You're too young to have your knee replaced."

I said, "Listen, dude. I have absolutely NOTHING to lose by having this surgery. Nothing, okay? I'm already wheelchair-bound. I have no life. And I DO NOT care what is allowable and what is not! I am DONE with my situation. Again, I have nothing to lose, but I have EVERYTHING to gain. Like, what if that surgery can get me out of this wheelchair? You don't understand. I'm so desperate right now that I will convince my parents to drive me down to Mexico, and we'll find somebody in the back of a van doing, you know, knee replacements for, you know, 50% off. I don't know. I don't care. I will do whatever it takes to have this surgery because I've done some research on it, and I feel like this is the ONLY option for me. If you don't perform the procedure, I'll find someone who will."

This went on for a few weeks, and he finally agreed to do the surgery for me. On June 29, 1994, I had my left knee operated on first because it was in worse condition. The surgery lasted several hours. I was five foot five going into this procedure. They had me standing up the day after I had my knee replaced, and I was now five foot seven. I had gained some inches because I had been sitting down for four years! SCIENCE! THE MORE YOU KNOW! Lol. Back then, you had to stay in the hospital for a whole week. My leg was put into a machine that basically bent and straightened my leg, exercising me. And I was doing extensive PT and OT just to get to where I could function. I lost a lot of blood, so I had to have two blood transfusions during that time.

After a few weeks, my bones started settling in, and I dropped down to a comfy height of five foot four. I started walking. I still had to use a walker, BUT I could walk around the house! I COULD WALK!!! I was independent again! I was no longer dependent on my family for everything. And now that I was able to stand up, I could see the "damage" that had been done while I was wheelchair-bound. Remember the lovely stretch marks I got after my initial diagnosis with the high prednisone use in a short amount of time? Well, apparently, when you are super thin and can no longer walk and then find yourself sitting for four years, you expand on your bottom. Yup, you guessed it, stretch marks. But it didn't matter. I didn't care anymore about things like that. I WAS WALKING AGAIN!!!!

We knew going into the next knee replacement surgery that my dad and I had the same blood type. We're the only two family members who are type O positive. So, four months after the first knee replacement, we donated for my following surgery to basically get my own blood back for the transfusions. My dad donated a pint. I donated a pint. I fainted after I came home from donating that pint, collapsing in the bathroom and nearly hitting my head on the toilet. I was scared that I had hurt my brand-new knee, but fortunately, I did not.

The left knee was done in June 1994, and I had the right knee done in November 1994. Oh, my gosh, it was absolutely amazing. I need to add that knee implants then were sort of made in a one-size-fits-all type of way. It's not like nowadays, where implants can be custom-built based on the size of the body frame that it's going into. I used to be very thin, never had heavy thighs or a heavy backside. But I had been sitting for four years! Then I got these knees, which were predominantly designed for older, bigger patients, so my legs had to "accommodate" for them and gradually got a bit thicker.

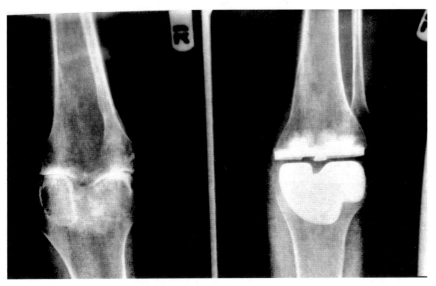

This is the only x-ray I could find from 1994. My right knee before and after the Total Knee Replacement surgery. I was 23 years old and in a wheelchair for 4 years.

It was like a ten-year curse had been lifted! Oh, wait. I totally forgot to mention this! I had my palm read at one point during wheelchair time, and the person reading my palm actually told me that I had a ten-year curse. This was around seven or eight years after my diagnosis. And then, ten years after diagnosis, I had my knees replaced. So, there was a part of me that was like, *Holy shit, was that real? Like, did someone curse our family? Did they curse me? And why? We aren't millionaires or even exceptionally well-off, so why the hell would anyone be jealous of our family?* There was no basis for it.

After those surgeries, for the first time in ten years, I felt like I had my life back; I felt like the whole world had become my oyster. I did my PT so religiously and diligently that my therapists and doctors were in awe at the speed of my recovery. I was absolutely determined to see this shit through! As far as I was concerned, I had been given the gift of life and normalcy, and I

WAS NOT about to mess this up! I walked, and I walked, and I walked EVERYWHERE! I was so grateful to have my life back.

For my 24th birthday that November, right after I had that second knee replaced, my sweet sister threw me a surprise birthday party. Initially, I had no idea what was going on. My friend had gotten me all dressed up and out of the house. I thought I was going to a fancy fashion show. When she drove me right back to my house, I was like, "Why did you bring me back here?"

She said, "Let's just run in real quick."

When I walked in, everyone yelled, "SURPRISE!" My whole family, including extended family and cousins, were all there! Mind you, I was a little bit disappointed that I wasn't going to the fashion show. Lol. It took a while for it to register, "THIS is your surprise birthday party, so shut up and enjoy it!"

I took all of my favorite drawings that I did while in a wheelchair to Michaels and got them all professionally custom framed. Apologies for the quality - they are still in frames. Here are a few of them:

Shading/blending with Prismacolors and stippling - a technique that uses small dots to create an image, pattern, or shading effect - with pen/ink were my favorite artistic techniques.

I rang in the new year, 1995, on my feet! I bought myself a snazzy black cane and named him Pierre. I had been given a second chance at life. And yes, after the first knee was replaced, I happily called my crush to inform him that I was finally walking again and wished him well in his marriage. Lol.

I decided to go back to UH. I had switched from business to graphic communications, and my hands were destroyed now, so I couldn't really do anything like artwork. So, I settled on psychology and went back to college in June 1995. I had the absolute most amazing time in college, mainly because I got to drive around in my brother's Nissan Stanza, which had two "12s" in the trunk (kickers) and an amp with a switch under the seat. Man, let me tell you something! Jazzy was rolling around the UH campus in my badass car – with my handicapped parking tag, no less, because, YES, I FINALLY got one – blasting my music, you know, UGK, Dre, Cube, NWA, DOC… just bumping on my speakers as I rolled up to my handicapped parking spots. I remember people looking at me like, "What the hell? Why is SHE parked in a handicapped spot?"

I was like, "Bring it on! Just ask me because I am not playing. Not anymore. I have been through hell and back. It has been ten years of suffering. Do NOT test me today, please. Or better yet, DO test me today. I'm always looking for a fight!" Lol. But I was so excited that I'd gotten a handicapped parking tag, gotten on disability, and had a second chance at life.

Because I was on disability, I was able to go to college for free. I can't even begin to tell you how big of a help that was for me because I would never have been able to afford it on my own. Social Security disability does not pay you a lot of money, but it gave me a sense of independence and hope that I could return to society and have a real life.

The very first thing I purchased with my disability check was a new stereo system (are you even surprised?) from JCPenney. It was a BADASS $800 Technics system with a turntable, receiver with equalizer, tall floor speakers, and BASS! As far as I was concerned, my new life was beginning, and I was super excited about it.

By this time, my treatments had gotten a whole lot better. I also joined a gym and started water aerobics, and I was on medications that were genuinely helping me and doing things that were beneficial to my joints. The damage had been done, though, so I knew I would probably need to have several surgeries later on.

I loved my time in college! I did SO WELL!! I made straight A's and got my GPA up from the nasty 2.0 range to a whopping 3.6! I graduated with honors from UH with a BA in psychology and a minor in sociology. I had intended to minor in Spanish and took almost every single class I needed for it, but when I walked into the very last class I needed, it was over. The class was Women in Hispanic Literature. EVERY SINGLE person in that class was a native Spanish speaker except for my Indian ass. The entire class was in Spanish, as were all the books and essays. I walked out of that classroom so fast and into my advisor's office and switched to sociology!

While studying psychology, I chose to be a research assistant and part of a research program studying women who had been dealing with domestic violence and its effects on their children. I ended up getting a job with them, becoming a research assistant at the Psychological Services Center, and I had a fantastic time meeting some amazing people. *Someday*, I thought, *I'm going to get my master's, and this is what I'm going to do for the rest of my life. Either go into abnormal child psychology or become a psychologist or maybe go into something like the School of Public Health.* I continued this job after graduating.

The very first thing I did upon graduating was move out of my parents' house. I simply needed to be on my own. I was so excited to have my independence! I actually moved out the week after I graduated. I moved into a super-cute two-bedroom apartment with my college bestie, and we had the time of our lives together! I didn't say anything to my parents about it until it was a done deal because I was scared that they would try to change my mind. I knew they wanted me to stay at home with them until I was married, but as far as I was concerned, I wasn't going to get married. Remember, I had been told my entire life that it wouldn't happen. So, what else was there for me, anyway?

Another opportunity that fell into my lap during this time was that I knew of a doctorate student who had a five-year-old autistic child. She and her husband had ten therapists on rotation to get him to a higher level of functioning. It was like having 24/7 therapy, and I was given the opportunity to be one of those therapists. I did it for about three or four months before I got so burnt out from the depression. I was already a little depressed due to health crap. Yes, I was excited about living on my own and walking, but it was still a challenge in terms of my health and juggling everything. At the same time, working in an environment where I was watching this beautiful kid who could not communicate with me was so incredibly sad. I felt that I couldn't help him, and it was heartbreaking.

Around this time, in 1999, they developed treatments for RA called "biologics," and Embrel was the very first. It was launched as an absolute game-changer in rheumatoid arthritis treatment. I was one of the first patients to receive it, and it was very helpful for me! Given the extent of the disease in my body, I was a unique case, which made me ideal for a guinea pig. The thing about these biologic treatments is that you have to self-inject. This was the first time in my life that I had to do the injections myself. I believe the dosing was once a week. I injected myself, and things were going fairly well. It was working for me!

So, I mentioned that I moved out of my parents' home a week after I graduated from the University of Houston and moved in with one of my best friends. She became my roommate, and we lived in this beautiful little complex in the Montrose area of Houston. It reminded me of *Melrose Place*. If you haven't seen the show, all the units surrounded a pool in the center. This one had a courtyard in the center, with all of our units surrounding it. It was really cute.

My roommate convinced me to quit my job as a therapist with this five-year-old autistic child. She said, "Dude, you've got to quit this job. I know that you want to do it because it's good for your resume and experience, but you're bringing that shit home. You're already struggling with your health. You do not want to add this burden." We're very good friends to this day. She's like my sister from another mister. We always say that one day, we're going to get together and write a book based on all of the things we did while we were roommates because we had so much fun together! I will not talk about it in this book just because it's too much. Maybe that'll be something on the radar later that she and I might do because we got into some shenanigans, man. Lol.

While we were living together, I had my right ankle fused. We lived in an upstairs unit, so I had to hobble up and down those stairs. We also went and saw Depeche Mode two days after my cast was removed from my foot. We pulled up to the OG Summit in Houston. Remember that venue before it got taken over by the megachurch? We parked right up front in handicapped parking. So, I went to Depeche Mode in a boot and stood the entire time for the concert. I was like, *It's Depeche Mode. I'm not sitting down.* I held onto the railing and danced, just jigging a little bit because I couldn't really move because of the boot on my foot.

We also started going to clubs together and dancing. We would go to house music clubs. The club that I got really into and just absolutely loved dancing at was called Spy. All the door people knew me, the bouncers knew me, and the DJs knew me. It kind of became an unpaid "job" for me, but they knew that I was coming to the club every single weekend. I had VIP passes, so I never had to pay to get in. It was just so much fun. I was just there to dance!

After Spy, I started going to Prague, and that became my home away from home. I just went to dance and experience the music and had so much

Taken after the Depeche Mode concert on November 18, 1998. If you look to the bottom left, you'll see my snazzy cane, "Pierre."

fun with that. The energy in a club filled with music that you love – there's no other feeling quite like it, not for someone who LOVES music and dancing as much as I do.

Around this time, I actually got an opportunity to go back to India again for the first time since my wheelchair time. It was amazing. One of my cousins was getting married, so my dad, my brother, and I flew out to India for her wedding. I kept thinking that it was going to be a magical experience because I hadn't been there in four years. This time, I wouldn't be in a wheelchair. Keep in mind that when you're in a wheelchair, you're seeing everything at eye level. Seeing it all while standing up gives you a completely different perspective.

Needless to say, the trip was incredibly emotional. During the wedding, my dad and his sister, my aunt, spoke with another attendee who informed my dad after seeing me that he would be "willing to marry" me despite everything. And yeah, my dad shared that news with me, including the phrase "willing to marry her." I lost it, and I did not speak to my dad for a few days. I feel guilty about it to this day because it wasn't his fault. He just wanted me to be happy, and this guy was, like, willing to marry me. I mean, what would you do? You know, you have a very conservative family that you grew up with, and they just want you to be happy. They want the best for their child. He wasn't doing anything malicious, but I wasn't for sale, and I wasn't desperate. I thought, *I am not chopped liver, and I don't need to be married. I'm perfectly fine. IF and WHEN I choose to get married, it will be on MY terms and with a person of my own choosing.* So, that was it. No more discussion about that.

When we returned home, I decided to take my chances with online dating. Back then, there wasn't really anything major. There were some matchmaking dating sites out there, but I don't remember what they were. I took my chances with Yahoo! Personals at first, and I did try to talk to Indian guys, but I didn't quite realize how incredibly shallow every single one of them was. I think I went out maybe two or three times with Indian guys. I didn't even meet some of them in person. Sometimes, I just spoke to them, and as soon as I mentioned rheumatoid arthritis, I never heard from them again, or they ghosted me.

I stayed at the UH job until 2000. From there, I went to the University of Texas Mental Sciences Institute and worked there for a few months. During this time, a new dating site emerged called Matchmaker, and I decided to give it a shot. At around the same time, I thought, *I really don't want to do psychology anymore. I'm not really into this anymore. I want to do something different, something that's happier and not so freaking depressing. I've had my fill of depressing shit in life. I need a change!* I also needed to make money. Clearly, there's no money to be made in psychology unless you get your master's or your PhD, and I didn't want to do it. I also didn't want to study for my GRE. I was already an older student because I'd lost four years of my life being in a wheelchair, and I wasn't going to study for a standardized test at that age.

One of my friends was looking at sales positions, so I decided to start looking at them, too. It just so happened I got an interview with the Art Institute of Houston, and I was like, *Come on, are you kidding me? This is where I wanted to go to college. And I have an opportunity to work with them now? Me? You can't be serious.* Long story short, I got the job and became a high school representative.

Around that same time, I met a guy on Matchmaker who would end up sweeping me off of my feet. On our very first date, he showed up late (strike one), he reeked of cigarette smoke (strike two), and when we got to the restaurant, he quite arrogantly said that he was going to "sweep me off of my feet and marry me" (strike three). Lol. Funny now, not so much back then.

Fast forward a few months, and we'd started dating. I broke up with him three times for various reasons, mostly because he was eight years younger than me. He was not Indian, and we didn't really have a ton of things in common. He was into heavy metal music, which, as you well know, is not my cup of tea. I'm your EDM, Depeche Mode girl. He smoked, and I was not a fan of that. And it was just like, why am I doing this? It didn't make any sense.

However, he was willing to quit smoking for me, and he wrote me the sweetest poems and letters, and he even wrote me a song! Most importantly, he ADORED me! He DID NOT care about my scars, my knees, my hands. He wanted me for me! Plain and simple. Come on! That was a no-brainer. So, we basically ended up together, and it was at that same time that I started my career at The Art Institutes. I'd just turned 30.

CHAPTER 8
DON'T LET ME DOWN

NEVER LET ME DOWN AGAIN
Depeche Mode

I was flying SO high during this time of my life!
I felt like I was marrying my best friend.
Taking the ride of my life with my best friend.
I never wanted to come down from this feeling.
I never wanted my feet to touch the ground.
Please don't let me down.

I'd met the man I would marry. We got engaged about a year after meeting. It was very whirlwind-esque because I chose to take him with me to my parents' house. I was moving from one place to another, and he was helping me collect some heavy things from my parents' house. I warned him that they were probably going to grill him and me, but we did it anyway. I needed his help. As soon we walked through the door, the questions started: "Who is this guy? Where is he from? What are his intentions? What are you going to do?"

I knew he was in love with me, and I loved him, too. He'd won me over! There was no formal engagement. We were at his parents' farm, and while sitting on the back patio, we simply decided to get engaged. I didn't want anybody else. He didn't want anyone else. So, we got engaged. We drove into Corpus Christi and got some cheap rings from a cool store in the mall, and that was it. We were engaged.

We were on cloud nine! I was able to accomplish something that everybody had told me I never would. The best thing about my fiancé was that he didn't care about the way my hands looked. He didn't care about all of the medications I was taking and that I had 12-inch scars on both legs. It didn't matter. He loved me for me. All the other guys, especially the Indian guys I had talked to, had always seemed to have some sort of an issue with my hands and the way that they looked. He never once said anything negative about them. He was just incredibly sympathetic, empathetic, and so sweet about the whole thing. It made me love him even more. Things seemed to be looking up. We set the date for our wedding and got married on April 20, 2002, which always makes me chuckle due to the irony later in life.

Shortly after this time, the wonderful medication that I was on, Embrel, went into a nationwide shortage. It may have been a worldwide shortage, actually, because the drug was very powerful, and they weren't able to manufacture it fast enough. I had to skip injections, and it was tanking my health. I was not feeling well, so I had to get on a different treatment. By that time, another treatment had popped up for rheumatoid arthritis: Remicade. Back then, you couldn't self-inject Remicade; it had to be administered through IV infusion. I don't know what my body did not like about that treatment, but every time they put the IV in and started the medication, I would get an allergic reaction right away. My heart would start racing, and I felt like I was going to die or faint. Eventually, we figured out that I needed to take Benadryl one hour before I got the treatment. They also needed to start the IV at a slow pace at first and then stop it after 15 minutes. After my body had calmed down, they would restart the drip at a slower pace. It took two hours for me to get my infusions. It was insane, but I needed some sort of relief.

This treatment started a year after we got married. When you're on these biologic medications, they are more effective when you take another medication with it, called methotrexate. This drug can cause spontaneous miscarriages, so it's very dangerous to get pregnant while on it. As far as I was concerned, I had been on so many different treatments, so many ulcers in my stomach, and other things that were just destroying my body that there was no way in hell I could ever even *get* pregnant. I wasn't on the pill during that time because of the treatment changes I had going on. I was taking too many drugs to keep track of. It was too much. My body needed a break, so I got off the pill.

I got pregnant.

I discovered I was pregnant in 2003 while I was on methotrexate. When that happens, the chances are VERY high that you're going to miscarry. I was shocked. This literally shook me to my core. It was such a difficult emotion to explain because, on the one hand, I was excited to learn that I could get pregnant, but on the other, I knew that the pregnancy wouldn't be viable. I was crushed. I knew I was going to lose the baby because of the methotrexate, so I freaked out. My husband was so supportive and so sweet during this whole time! I called my rheumatologist's office, and they told me to go ahead and plan the D&C. Then I called Planned Parenthood and scheduled the procedure for the following Friday.

Why didn't I have it as soon as I knew I needed to have it done? I had already started spotting. Something else was going on. I also had jury duty, and I'd been selected for the jury. From April 8 to April 10, I sat on a jury for a criminal trial, and I had a miscarriage during proceedings. I was cramping and in pain. The morning after I finished jury duty, I went to Planned Parenthood and got everything cleaned out. That experience was GUT-WRENCHING! It was such a double-edged sword. My husband and I were devastated that we'd lost our child, but there was a small glimmer of hope that we could have our own child, and the experience brought us even closer together.

We'd discussed having children at the beginning of our relationship. I'd always told him that there was probably no chance I could ever get pregnant, and he was okay with that. He only wanted me. It didn't matter to either of us if we ever had kids. We had already settled on that. But when this happened, it took us by surprise, both in a positive and negative way. But we had to cross that bridge later because I needed to start fixing my damaged joints.

Before getting pregnant, I had already had a surgery consultation to fix my hands and have all of my MCP knuckles replaced. These are the knuckles that connect your palm to your fingers. They were all destroyed and needed to be replaced in both of my hands. In May, I had all of the knuckles replaced in my right hand, and they put in plastic implants. My surgeon used stitches that were supposed to self-dissolve, but they did not. So, the following year, two weeks before I went in to have the left hand done, he had to remove the stitches that had never dissolved in the right hand.

My husband and I started having serious conversations about getting pregnant and if we wanted to risk it. It is a tremendous risk for a woman with a severe autoimmune disease to get pregnant. There's an 80% chance that the woman will go into remission during pregnancy due to the hormones and changes happening. However, there's a 20% chance that she won't, which means I could be bedridden for the entire pregnancy. It was a lot to consider. Plus, we were in a ton of debt. We couldn't afford a child.

If we wanted to have a child, we first needed to get out of debt, so we moved in with my parents for about four months. Then we started talking more seriously about having a child. After much thought and deliberation, we decided that I would stop taking all my medications. To even get pregnant, you have to detox from methotrexate for a minimum of four months. I was terrified about being in the 20% of women who don't go into remission, but we decided it was a risk we were both prepared to take.

Those four months were absolute hell. Thankfully, we were living with my parents at that time, so I had help. My mom always cooked, and I was in really good hands. We didn't tell anyone that we were going to try to have a baby. I didn't want my family to get worried about me being off of my meds. I was in excruciating pain and swelling. I was hurting so badly, but I stayed focused on the goal.

My husband and I also discussed what we would do if I didn't get pregnant right away because I could only stay off of my meds for so long before my health would suffer more. We decided that if I didn't get pregnant after four months, we would call it a day and not try to do it because it was a tremendous struggle for me. I was allowed to take Tylenol and steroids, prednisone, and you know how I feel about prednisone. I really didn't want to be on it very long. It was very scary.

During this time frame, I also had surgery on my feet to fix all of my toes. I had them straightened at the same time! On both feet! I know, so stupid. But I was desperate to try to get pregnant. I was already 34 and high risk due to both age and disease progression. What possessed me to go and have this surgery while I was detoxing from medications, I don't know. All I know is that I wanted to be in the best possible shape for my child. I wanted to be able to hold and walk around with my baby, so I needed my joints to work for me.

Fast forward to the four-month marker, and I found out that I was pregnant. I'm not even kidding. Almost on the dot! I went to a meeting for The Art Institutes in Dallas and found out I'd made President's Club. I had been considering leaving that position and seeking something elsewhere to get more money, but now I decided to stay put. I went home, and we celebrated the President's Club win, and that's when I got pregnant. We did the pregnancy test at my in-laws' farm, and they were the first ones we told. Their reaction was quite underwhelming. Lol. They were nervous about it due to my health, so their reaction was not what we were expecting at all. It made me feel sad because they didn't seem very supportive or happy about it. My family, on the other hand, was absolutely ELATED! They were so excited and happy for us.

My husband and I went to a Depeche Mode concert while I was pregnant, and I was terrified about the noise because our seats were so close to the stage.

I called my OBGYN and asked, "Is this going to be okay? Am I compromising my child's hearing or anything like that?" They told me I would be perfectly fine, and that eased my fears. That was such a special experience, singing and dancing to Depeche Mode with my miracle baby growing in my belly.

Soon after I found out I was pregnant, I also learned that my dad had prostate cancer. It was so sad. It always seemed that when something good happened, something bad would happen soon after. Apparently, he'd known about the cancer for a while. He had been diagnosed with ulcerative colitis a few years prior, and now he'd been diagnosed with prostate cancer. Unfortunately, the radiation therapy was making his ulcerative colitis worse, and he wasn't doing too well. Also, because I was pregnant, he wasn't allowed to go near me, so I had to stay six feet away from him.

At this time, I was very involved with the Arthritis Foundation. My rheumatologist had put me in touch with the foundation, and they were getting ready to have their arthritis walk. They heard my story that I had been in a wheelchair for four years, and they wanted me to be their "Walk Hero" for 2006. What a huge honor! They had an adult "Walk Hero" and a juvenile "Walk Hero." The juvenile "Walk Hero" was the child of one of my good friends (we're still friends to this day). I also recorded a radio interview with 104 KRBE, and the *Houston Chronicle* wrote a whole article about me as the Arthritis Foundation's 2006 Walk Hero. It was a pretty big deal. Unfortunately, I wasn't able to attend the arthritis walk because I had given birth three weeks before.

I had to be induced three weeks early, but I had the most amazing pregnancy. I did go into a temporary remission, and I was the happiest pregnant woman! I was so incredibly blessed! I was enjoying the pregnancy as much as possible because it was the first time I had been off of all these medications and drugs for the longest time. And I was doing pretty well! Surprisingly, I was able to give birth vaginally. Apparently, my hips were healthy enough for me to be able to give birth that way. The only issues with my pregnancy were, one, that I was high-risk because of the RA and, two, that

I was high-risk because I was 34 and had low amniotic fluid, so I had to be induced three weeks early.

My miracle baby was born on April 25, 2006. My sweet baby girl. Oh, my God. I thought I loved my husband. The overwhelming sense of love and protection that emanated from every single fiber of my being for this child was unreal. This was my baby. I'd made this baby. This baby was a true miracle. I immediately put a force field of protection around her.

I was not taking any chances with my child and my child's health. We joined the cord blood registry. I made sure that they cut her umbilical cord and put that specimen in a bottle, and it is still sitting in the Cord Blood Registry in Tucson, Arizona, right now. I pay a yearly fee to store her stem cells. If my child ever has any type of autoimmune anything, I have that in place to do whatever is necessary to help her. I already knew it was too late for me, but I was not taking any chances with my child.

To this day, I do a full blood panel on my child every single year during annual exams, checking for RA and any other autoimmune disease. After she was born, I made sure that nobody went near her or touched her without washing their hands thoroughly. If you need to put a mask on, do it. If you're not feeling well, don't touch my kid. Don't even go near my kid. I know it made our families annoyed, but I didn't care. All that mattered was my baby. She was my responsibility, and I took that responsibility seriously.

On top of everything else, while I was on maternity leave, I got promoted to associate director, which was fantastic because I've always been incredibly ambitious. More money, please! I wanted to provide all of the things for my child that I didn't have growing up. The only downside to the promotion was that the amount of traveling would increase. But we needed the money, and I truly LOVED the traveling. With The Art Institutes, I got to travel all over Texas, Louisiana, Oklahoma, Arizona, Minnesota, New Mexico, Colorado, Kansas, Missouri, Nevada, California, Oregon, Washington, North Dakota, and South Dakota. And I trained in North Dakota. Who trains for a job in Fargo, North Dakota? Well, I did. Lol. That was the very first place that I flew out to when I trained for the job in 2000. Later in my career, I would acquire the entire territory of Canada. I loved this job so much.

What I regret the most about all the traveling that I did was that I didn't get to really enjoy the places that I went to because I was traveling alone. As a disabled woman, unable to really defend myself, I didn't feel comfortable going sightseeing or eating by myself in public. Now that I'm older and healthier, I feel like I just want to go back to some of these places and explore. But I loved traveling for my job. I really enjoyed my alone time and getting out of the house. I loved my baby, and I loved my husband. I loved being in that environment, and I missed them terribly when I was gone, but I also loved my independence. Being away helped me mentally, too, because I got a break. When I flew, I always had my headphones with me and listened to music or read books on my Kindle (BEST INVENTION EVER for those of us with severe hand issues). That was my solace. It was everything for me.

After I gave birth to my child, I didn't realize how quickly the RA would hit me. I was only able to breastfeed her for four months, maybe five, and then my body tanked. I was in really bad shape. The RA was worse than it had been before I got pregnant. I felt like I'd been in a head-on collision with a truck. My rheumatologist warned me that this might happen and it might get worse, and I knew the remission would be very short-lived as it was only due to the pregnancy hormones. Once they were gone, my body tanked.

I was hurting so much that they put me on Cymbalta, which is an antidepressant that's also used to treat fibromyalgia to help with random joint aches and pain in your body. I was also on a new biologic injection called Humira. And can you believe that the manufacturer of Humira asked me to stay on it during my pregnancy so they could follow the progress? I said, "Absolutely NOT!" I had ZERO intention of staying on any dangerous drugs while pregnant.

Postpartum, I ended up on three or four different medications just for rheumatoid arthritis. The pain was unbelievable. The swelling was unbelievable. I wish I would have been an advocate for therapy back then because I REALLY needed it. I was so fucking tired and in so much pain. I needed to be a mom, I needed to be a wife, I needed to support my family and keep working, but I felt like I was slowly dying. My body was SCREAMING at me. And I know all of this was taking a toll on my husband too. It was a lot. Caretakers deserve to be heard.

Then I got another promotion, this time to director. There were two good things about this promotion. One was the money, which was amazing! The second was that my daily travel went down considerably because now I was managing teams. I was also wearing three different hats because not only did they decide that I would manage the high school rep team, but they also launched the business development program that year. I had four business development reps, the most in the nation, and I was also responsible for the presentation design team. In fact, I was the leader of the presentation design team. Wearing those three hats while juggling rheumatoid arthritis, chronic pain, and fatigue and raising a family, I felt like I was in a downward spiral.

I loved my husband deeply, and although I was the primary breadwinner, I was okay with it—I even liked it. Besides, he took such good care of me! I know all of this was overwhelming for him too. We could not afford for me not to work. And let's be clear: I didn't want to stop working. I was VERY ambitious in my career and kept wanting to move up. That's why I never stopped. I was also scared of being in a wheelchair again, and I would do everything I could to ensure that NEVER happened to me again.

I also started getting crazy sick during that time. I realized around 2008 that I was having major thyroid issues.

The thing about rheumatoid arthritis – and any type of autoimmune disease – is that whatever happens in your body during pregnancy, your body loves it, the autoimmune stuff loves it, and your immune system loves it. But once the pregnancy is over and all those beautiful hormones are gone, your body is like, *Where the hell did all that go?* Also, if you already have an autoimmune disease, you are prone to getting more, as your immune system is already compromised. My body was already struggling with RA, so it was like, *Sure, come on in. We've got a party over here in this body.*

I was diagnosed with Hashimoto's hypothyroidism. My body was pissed. They put me on Synthroid for the thyroid. I was on all the other medications for rheumatoid arthritis, and my liver was not happy with that combination. All of a sudden, I started itching like crazy, I got diarrhea, and I turned yellow. I literally turned yellow. I was in Austin for our kickoff meeting to start the school year, and I couldn't stop scratching or going to the bathroom, and I turned yellow. It was such a bizarre week!

When I got home, we were hanging out with my family, and they said, "You are very yellow. The whites of your eyes are totally yellow."

"I need to go to the emergency room," I told them. "Something's wrong."

We went to the ER, and it's a funny story because, when I walked into the ER, they asked me, "What are you here for?"

"I'm here because I'm yellow," I replied. "I don't know what else to say to you."

"Oh my gosh, yeah, you're jaundiced." So, liver toxicity is what was happening. Apparently, the combination of Cymbalta and another RA medication they'd put me on called Arava, which is comparable to methotrexate, was destroying my liver.

I was told I had primary biliary cirrhosis of my liver. WHAT? And it had also started affecting my lungs. They did an X-ray and found an 11-millimeter mass in my lungs and said I might have interstitial lung disease. It's never been confirmed, though, and there is a semi-funny story around that. I had a full-on bronchoscope and everything, and I went to my appointment a week or two later to get the results from that test at the world-renowned Houston Medical Center. If you've ever tried to park your car in the Methodist parking garages (Smith or Scurlock Tower – pick your poison), you know EXACTLY what I'm about to say. I went around that parking garage so many times, loop-de-loop-de-loop, and I was like, "I'm done." I couldn't find a spot, so I went home. On the way, I called the doctor's office and said, "I had to leave. I'm sorry. I couldn't find a parking spot, and clearly, I missed my appointment. I'll just have to call y'all later and schedule something."

I was juggling so many things: my job, my family, my pain, two lesions in my liver, jaundice, and diarrhea. I wasn't even thinking about my lungs. I never confirmed whether I had interstitial lung disease or not. I don't think I had it because I'm pretty sure I would have known by now if I did, but I never went for that follow-up.

Slowly but surely, I grew resentful. I felt like I was falling apart. Don't get me wrong, I had A LOT of support from my husband, but he basically transitioned from my husband to my caretaker. I got to a point where it was nearly impossible to hold my daughter because of my hands. It's very challenging to hold your child when you have plastic implants in your hands or when you are suffering a flare-up. It hits everywhere. It wasn't just in my fingers; it was in my elbows, my shoulders, and my neck. When it came to holding a child who was bouncing around, I couldn't do that for very long.

Sadly, I always felt like my child was closer to her dad than she was to me. While this broke my heart, it also gave me solace, as *at least she has him when I'm so tired all the time.* But I did resent that a little bit, the fact that I couldn't hold my child, get on the floor and play with her, or quit my job and stay home because we needed my salary. But as I mentioned, I loved my job. It was my sanity. And I WANTED this! Otherwise, I would have gone crazy. I HAD to work for my own peace of mind. I wasn't about to quit or anything. That was out of the question.

Shortly after that, my father-in-law passed away. It was a no-brainer for me to invite my mother-in-law to live with us because that's what you do in Indian culture. You don't leave your in-laws and parents to live on their own when they have a big life change like that. You bring them in to live with you. I was also hopeful that she might help me, too. I needed help. We needed help. If she could do some of the cooking, help with the cleaning and watching the baby, and maybe even allow us to go out and have our own date nights and stuff, that would be a huge blessing.

Well, we invited her to come live with us, and it was good. Don't get me wrong. I loved my mother-in-law so much, but it wasn't exactly what I had initially thought it might be. The house that we were in at the time was too small, so we ended up upgrading. My mother-in-law helped us financially with the down payment, so we upgraded to what was essentially our dream home. We were paying her back. And we were all living together harmoniously. Things were great in the beginning.

I don't know if I mentioned this before, but my husband is an atheist, so spirituality during my marriage was almost non-existent. I wasn't super religious anyway, but because of his lack of spiritual insight, I CHOSE to forgo my own spirituality. I take full responsibility. I still did my prayers, and I still had faith in my heart. I was like, *You know what? My higher power knows what's in my heart. It's cool.*

I did this because I didn't want to have any tension in my marriage. I thought, *Okay, you are an atheist, and I'm Sikh. We'll make this work because we love each other, right?* But I wasn't practicing, and I didn't really want to go to church anyway because I didn't want to see some of the people who said mean things to me or be nosy about my life. I just wanted to live a happy life, stay away from gossip, and shield my child from it, too.

Spirituality was very challenging for me during this time because I didn't know what to do with it. I wanted to try and raise my child in a spiritual way, but I also didn't want to have any marital issues. We had agreed not to push any religion on our child and that we'd let her make up her own mind as she got older. I realize now how much I was truly missing out on! I wish I had leaned on my faith more, but I didn't. I can't go back and change the past anyway, so it is what it is at this point.

Our marriage was wonderful. I felt so supported by him! He was a good husband and an even better dad to our daughter. We didn't have a honeymoon after we got married, and our first official trip together happened to be 12 years after marriage, so we decided to take our child with us. We decided to go to Puerto Vallarta in 2014, and it was absolutely amazing. We should have been doing things for us, just the two of us, all along, but we didn't. I was also averaging one surgery per year. I didn't have time. Even then, we took our child with us. In hindsight, that was probably not the best idea, but it's too late to change it now, right? Let that shit go.

By this time, I'd already had the knuckles replaced in both hands. I had to have my right ankle re-fused because it wasn't done properly the first time around. My ankle had been completely reconstructed and fully fused to where I was even more limited in my motion, so I had to be very careful with the workouts that I did. I was also having issues with lumps in my breast from breastfeeding. Even though I only breastfed for a limited time, it was causing cysts in my breast. I had a biopsy in 2012, another one in 2013, and then had a mass removed in 2014, right after we came back from Puerto Vallarta. I was averaging about five cortisone shots per year in my shoulders, elbows, hands, wrists, and fingers. I was an absolute mess, and I was still working. I think I went on short-term disability once a year!

Despite my many surgeries, I still managed to excel at my job. I was one of the top-producing directors, and I got so many awards and accolades! I LOVED my team so much! We were the "Houston Honey Badgers," and then we became the "Screaming Easels." Lol! I loved my fellow directors, our senior directors, and our VP. We were a FAMILY! It was a once-in-a-lifetime career with SO MUCH support! I was so incredibly blessed! But things were starting to get shaky in the world of non-profit colleges.

Things were starting to get more and more shaky at home with my mother-in-law. She moved out, and we realized we couldn't stay in our dream home any longer. It was simply too expensive so we had to downsize. In 2015, I was laid off from The Art Institutes and immediately rehired as the staff was being reduced. During my rehire, I acquired Canada as my territory. It was going to be the MOST traveling I would ever do in this job. I spent 15 weeks on the road during the 2015–2016 school year!

When we downsized our home, I was not happy with the house that we ended up in because it wasn't what I would have picked for my family, but we were in a time crunch. It was too small and was an older home. I didn't like that. Our old house, our dream house, sold so quickly that we didn't have much choice. A house was listed, and the realtor was putting the sign up. I saw it, drove by immediately, and said, "Pull it off the market. We're taking it." We had to. We were desperate.

After moving to our new house, we met some amazing friends and decided to plan a joint trip to Disney World before I had major surgery in 2016 on my right shoulder. My job was still up in the air. They'd already reduced staff the year before when I'd been laid off the first time, but the rumor was that everything was about to explode.

If we were going to do the Disney trip, we had to do it now. I literally flew back from Vancouver, where I'd been for work, and we left for Disney two days later. My daughter and my friend's child were best friends, so both couples and kids went. The trip was great fun, but it was also very challenging. Oh, my God, the amount of walking that I did. I was a trooper as much as I could be, but there was SO MUCH WALKING! I was already slow to begin with, so I would tell everybody else not to wait for me and that I would catch up. I had to take breaks and sit down. By the fifth day of park walking, when we went to the Magic Kingdom, I had to suck it up and use a wheelchair. I hated doing it, but by that point, I was struggling too much. Despite the fact that I was hurting so badly and my feet and ankles were so swollen, we had an amazing time.

As soon as we came back home, it was time for me to have my shoulder replaced. My right shoulder was so far gone that they weren't even able to do a regular total shoulder replacement. They had to do what's called a reverse total shoulder. The difference is that when your rotator cuff is completely destroyed, you don't have that range of motion anymore, so the ball socket is placed in reverse.

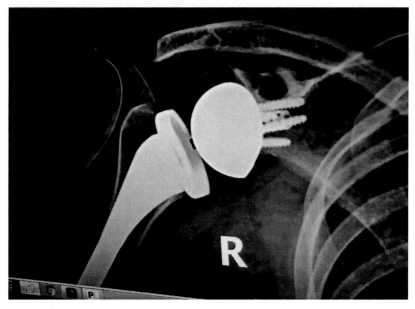

X-ray of my right shoulder after the Reverse Total Shoulder Replacement surgery.

Two weeks after my shoulder replacement, I finally lost my dream job with The Art Institutes. Permanently.

I was GUTTED!

CHAPTER 9

MY WORLD FALLS APART

HALO

Depeche Mode

Just like that, everything fell apart.
My world was crumbling down around me.
I didn't know it at the time, but it would be worth it.
In the end.

I had just had a reverse total shoulder replacement done. Of ALL the surgeries I had had up to this point, THIS one had the MOST painful recovery. I was crying so much! It hurt SO BADLY! And I knew the job situation was very iffy. I had just finished all of the monthly reviews for my entire team and all of my reps, and I was ONE-HANDED because I'd just had a brand-new shoulder joint installed.

Then, two weeks after my shoulder was replaced, I lost my job. My whole department was dissolved. The entire high school team was on a conference call, and they let everybody go… the entire department, almost three hundred people. We were given 24 hours to clean out our laptops and ship them back before we were shut out. It was so intense and utterly devastating. It was so callous. So disgusting. So disrespectful. After serving the company for 16 years as a loyal employee, in the blink of an eye, it was all gone. And they didn't even care. We lost all access, and everything was shut down.

I was devastated. It was the best job for me, for my health. I got to work from home, pick my baby up from school, schedule travel around my family time, and schedule doctor's appointments and surgeries that coincided with my baby's school schedule. It was perfect.

To this day, I look at my beautiful awards. I still have a few that I've held onto. I got so many awards y'all. I was an amazing rep. I was a badass director. I was the spreadsheet queen! I was SOOOO good at my job. I knew it like the back of my hand. That's why I didn't want it to end. I could do it with my eyes closed. And it was such good money. It was *enough* money. I had company cars, and then we switched to stipends. They paid for my home office. It was a beautiful set-up.

Most importantly, I got to work from home. I didn't have to commute. I was able to be at home with my child. I had her in daycare, but I got to pick her up whenever I wanted. If I didn't have a lot of meetings in a day, I would just keep her at home with me. It was the best job for me and us. It was the best job for my health.

The shoulder replacement was so painful. I struggled SO MUCH with the post-op. I was having a difficult time with PT, and then I had to stop it early due to the job loss. I got a measly severance package for my 16 years of service, which was laughable. I had had RA for so many years that, with each surgery, it was taking me longer and longer to heal, and it was too much. When would this stop? Would it ever stop? I should have listened to my body. My body had been telling me for several years prior to this surgery and prior to my layoff, "You've got to slow it down." Shit, I was averaging one surgery and five cortisone shots a year. It's unbelievable.

I should have applied for disability at this point, but we couldn't afford it. I got unemployment, ended PT early because I lost my insurance coverage, and started applying for jobs and interviewing. Let me repeat that. I'd JUST had my shoulder replaced, and I was interviewing for jobs while I was barely able to use my right arm. I would cry in the car on the way to interviews. I didn't wear the sling to the interviews. I just wore it in the car while I drove, and then I would take it off before I went into the interviews because I didn't want the employer to think anything was wrong with me and discriminate.

I debated with myself: *I'm in a different place now than I was when I got that job with The Art Institutes 16 years ago. Now, do I need to tell people the level and severity of my disability? Shit, this changes things. My boss and HR at The Art Institutes were AWESOME with my health and accommodations. Who else is going to be that supportive?*

Then I thought, *No, I shouldn't have to tell anybody.* I knew what I was capable of, but I was terrified because what were the odds I was going to get a job again that would let me work from home and give me the same level of autonomy to schedule doctor visits and pick my baby up from school? My baby was about to start middle school now. This was the time in her life when she REALLY needed me! I needed to be there; I wanted to be there! What if I had to commute? How the hell was I going to commute to a job and drive daily?

I started shutting down mentally, physically, and spiritually. I was losing my damn mind. I went into a *very* dark place. I was very much struggling to find any positive in my life at this point. The happy-go-lucky Jasmine everyone knew and loved in previous chapters, by this point, was very resentful, very angry, just pissed off at the world, didn't want to be alive, didn't want to exist. It was incredibly challenging to figure out how I was going to move forward from this point. I took solace in knowing that I was going to be unemployed for several weeks, so I had a little bit of time, a buffer, to figure my shit out, get through this recovery, and get my shoulder up and running. At least unemployment would provide some income. And I had SO MUCH love and support from my husband and child!

Then I told myself, *Okay, I got this. I can certainly find something else that I'm going to be really good at.* I tried reaching out to the companies that made the implants that I have in my body. Zimmer is the company that made my knees. I reached out to those fools so many times. I told them, "Who better to sell your product than the person walking around with the implants inside of them?" They didn't even bother to respond to me! They wouldn't even acknowledge my applications, resume, and badass cover letter telling them my story. I was so disappointed. At least acknowledge me, right? But whatever. It is what it is – their loss.

After a few weeks, I got a random sales job and accepted it for the sake of getting a job, but it only lasted two or three weeks because they were so incredibly unethical. I will NOT mention their name here because they are still around today, but the amount of lying I was expected to do was NOT gonna happen! Lol. Let's just say that they had a very questionable call script that I was NOT willing to repeat. After that, I became a bit more selective about where I applied.

During this entire time, I was still struggling with my health, both physical and mental, and with the fact that the lease for our house, which none of us were happy in, was going to be up. We needed another place to live. I believe the shoulder replacement was when my husband lost his job, too. Thankfully, he found another position, and this one actually paid him the highest salary he'd ever gotten during our marriage with excellent benefits. That was great, but we were still trying to figure out how this was going to work. I could not survive without insurance! With my medical shit? And we still needed me to be at a particular salary so that we could enjoy the quality of life we were used to.

Here's where I was at this time in my medical journey and why I should have applied for disability at this point and also started therapy. Quick recap: By the beginning of 2017, I'd had 21 surgeries, five autoimmune diagnoses, and over 30 cortisone shots. I only started keeping track of the shots in 2004. I'm sure there are so many that I've missed.

To say I was exhausted would be an understatement. But I wasn't the only one. My husband was exhausted too! It was taking a toll on our family.

Meanwhile, I went to a job interview, and it was a position that would have been perfect if it was an at-home position. Sadly, it was not, but it was right up my alley because it was under the psychological umbrella, and my degree is in psychology. I took the job, but I had to commute. It paid really well and had amazing benefits, so I had no choice. I knew I had to drive from my house in Pearland all the way to the Galleria area in Houston proper. And if you're not familiar with Houston, it's massive, the fourth-largest city in the U.S.

My commute was an hour long, minimum, in the morning, sometimes an hour and 30 minutes depending on traffic/accidents/idiots, and an hour to an hour and a half back home in the evening. I felt so incredibly guilty taking this job because I wasn't at home anymore for my child. By the time I got home from work, I was dead to the world. I had to get up at 5 a.m. I'd never gotten up that early on a daily basis. Well, I did get up early like that for The Art Institutes when I traveled, but I knew my day was going to be over by the afternoon, and it wasn't ON A DAILY BASIS.

I could no longer make doctor appointments during work time. I had to take PTO and schedule two to three appointments in a day. I had NO CHOICE but to get up at 5 a.m. daily. My body was in an UPROAR! The hours were regular, 8 a.m. to 5 p.m., not including the commute, but by the time I got home, I was useless. Yes, I enjoyed the job, and yes, I enjoyed the people, but my body was starting to scream at me, and the resentment that I had was killing me. I wish I could have stopped working. I was so fucking tired.

The commute was killing me. All of it was killing me. But I truly enjoyed the job – until I didn't enjoy the job anymore. I was hired to launch their business development program. The first few months were GREAT! Then things took a turn, and it seemed like I couldn't do anything right. It seemed like everything I did was being questioned. Keep in mind that I came from an organization where I was one of the top performers as a rep and one of the top directors. My team loved me, and I loved them so much! We were a family! We still are! I LOVE my AI PEEPS! I was abundantly awarded and received so many accolades. AND I was the spreadsheet queen, and everyone knew it. Go to Jasmine if you want to learn about organization and multitasking. She is a beast! She is the queen of that stuff! Spreadsheets? Oh, my God, that was like my passion. I freaking loved them.

But now I'd gone from being valued and endeared to not being able to do anything right. What? My brain imploded. It's so hard for me to put into words what that did to me mentally. It was brutal. I was already dying mentally because of the depression that I had from losing my dream job. Then, my health started tanking. No surprise. My body was pissed that I was doing this job when I should have been at home, HEALING. I was questioning myself and doubting my abilities. I felt like a total loser! Imposter syndrome much? My resume is badass! But I felt as though it was all a lie. I had ZERO confidence in myself and my abilities. I TANKED!

Honestly, I should have been in therapy after I lost the AI job and struggled with my mental health. I should have been in therapy all along, but I wasn't. I didn't have time for it anyway, so it wouldn't have mattered. My supervisor and I just clashed. She wasn't happy with or supportive of my work. Everything I did was questioned. I was struggling. I was diagnosed with high blood pressure. My heart was always racing. My Apple Watch would alert me ALL DAY LONG! I'm not exaggerating. ALL DAY LONG: "Your heart rate is skyrocketing. Chill out, Jasmine. Calm down. Breathe, breathe, breathe."

I'm surprised I didn't have a heart attack. Remember when I was in the fifth and sixth grades and getting bullied? I would wake up with that gut-wrenching anxiety and a knotted-up stomach because I didn't want to go to school. Well, now I didn't want to go to work. That was happening HERE! At this job! As an ADULT! What in the actual fuck? It was the exact same feeling. I felt like I was being bullied all over again. My stomach started hurting so badly. I started having issues with my gut. I started having diarrhea for no reason. Internally, I was shutting down. I was barely talking to my family. I was barely talking to my friends because the commute was taking up my entire time. By the time I got home, I was dead to the world. I stopped spending time with my husband and child.

By the time I got home, I was in so much pain and just so done with life. I would go home, take a shower, get changed, eat dinner, and then go to bed. That was my schedule. Rinse and repeat. Maybe we would watch something together as a family – one or two episodes of a series was all I could really handle – and then I had to go into my bedroom no later than 7-8 p.m. and lie down on my heating pad.

It stung me so badly to hear my child and my husband sitting on the couch in the living room, laughing and enjoying each other's company while I was in the bedroom recovering. I wanted to be out there with them. I didn't know what was happening to me. I felt like I was completely useless to them both. Hell, I couldn't even help myself. How the hell was I supposed to help them? Thankfully, the job that my husband had allowed him to work from home, so at least one of us was there.

During this time, my husband and I went to a Depeche Mode concert, and it was the first time my daughter went with us. It was supposed to be a special moment, and it absolutely WAS! But I was so stressed during the show because I had to go to work the next day. I couldn't even enjoy that moment *fully* with my family. I hated that I didn't get to enjoy that moment as fully as I wanted to SO MUCH because of a job.

I started lying on a heating pad because I was hurting so bad, and it slowly became my crutch, my solace, my "security blanket." And the stomach pains didn't get any better. I had already been diagnosed with high blood pressure and had an elevated heart rate. I had three cortisone shots, two of them in my elbow and one in my shoulder, all within weeks of each other, just because of the commute back and forth. Oh, and I had a tonsillectomy. Lol. How can I forget? My snoring was getting really bad again, and my ENT said the only thing left to do was remove my tonsils because they'd already done several turbinectomies over the last few years (three of them – two surgical and one using audio waves). This all happened within months of starting that job.

Eventually, even holding the steering wheel became a massive challenge. It was killing my arms. I had a sporty car back then, an Acura ILX. It was a beautiful royal blue A-spec edition. I loved that car. My husband had an Acura TLX, so we switched cars because the TLX steering wheel was more manageable and easier to move, and that car also had push buttons for the shifter. I couldn't use the regular shifter in my ILX anymore. My hand and arm simply couldn't squeeze and pull the handle anymore.

There were days where I would cry all the way to work, cry all the way home, and hide my tears from my family. I was taking a painkiller and muscle relaxer *every single night* for several years, but now I couldn't afford to skip any doses. I needed to sleep without pain and wake up without pain. Sometimes, I had to take the pills during the day after I got to work. My God, it was SO MUCH SHIT! Prior to the tonsillectomy, I was getting throat infections. Then, after the tonsillectomy, I got the flu. TWICE – back to back! I was like, what is going on here? It's absolutely laughable. It was because of my environment! I was working in an office filled with germs, and my immune system LOVES a good illness/disease party. We already know that from my story thus far. Lol. I was only at this job for 14 months before I got SO SICK.

So, if you're keeping track, three cortisone shots in 14 months, high blood pressure diagnosis, elevated heart rate, tonsillectomy, and back-to-back flu. Then, I had to have surgery on my left elbow. It never stopped. There was too much debris, broken bones, and shards inside my elbow, and a nodule had formed on the bottom of my elbow that made it extremely painful to put my arm down on a table or my desk without it hurting. The surgeon did a synovectomy, where you vacuum out the debris, remove arthritic parts, and also remove the nodule. The nodule most likely formed because I was sitting at a desk five days a week and also laying my left arm down on the armrest in the car while in traffic. Because of my lack of a good range of motion, I had to have my arms on my desk for support for my hands/wrists while working on a computer. Sitting in that position for 14 months was destroying my hands even more. This was the second time I'd had a nodule in that same spot on my elbow. The first time was immediately after my knee replacements in 1994.

I was struggling so much. I could not catch a break at all. Then, the stomach pain started getting worse. On March 31, 2018, I was lying in bed watching the movie *Sing* with my daughter, and I felt like my gut ruptured. This is a horrific and awful memory that, sadly, I remember all too well. I went to the bathroom, and my body folded in half from the excruciating pain in my colon and gut. It was worse than any other pain I had ever had in my entire life. I was literally doubled over in pain, sweating, and having the WORST diarrhea, and IT WOULD NOT STOP. I thought it was food poisoning initially, but then I thought, *This is not food poisoning because I'm not nauseous or throwing up.* This was all in my gut. The only feeling in my life that ever came close to these kinds of cramps was when I was giving birth and the awful contractions. It was simply HORRIFYING. And nothing stopped the pain. I stayed in the bathroom for over an hour. I took everything I had in my arsenal, but NOTHING helped.

My husband and my baby took me to the ER, where the IV with morphine finally made the pain go away. I was so scared. And I know my husband and daughter were scared too! They did an MRI, and I was told I had acute colitis but needed to have an official colonoscopy done by my GI to find out what was going on. Keep in mind that I'd JUST started this job 14 months ago, and the number of health issues that arose during this time was stupid insane! Hell, I still had the stitches in my elbow from the surgery I had a week prior. Now, I was sitting in the ER, finding out that I had acute colitis. What? WHAT THE FUCK was happening to me? That was the same thing that my dad had, ulcerative colitis, and I knew the struggles that he had, so I was like, *No, please, God, no. Surely, this can't be real. This can't be happening right now. Please, no more. I can't do this anymore. I'm so tired. I'm so exhausted already. I need all of this to go away. I DON'T NEED ANY MORE. PLEASE.*

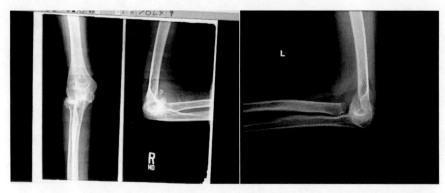

*The x-ray on the left is my elbow BEFORE any surgery. Bone on bone. I had a radial head
excision on both elbows in 2013–three months apart. On the right is my left elbow after the
synovectomy prior to the ER visit for the colitis.*

I decided in the ER that this was the final straw, I had to quit my job. I just couldn't do it anymore. I would find something else where I could work from home, and we'd figure it out. So, when I got back from the ER, I wrote my resignation letter. My beautiful baby girl had a choir recital that week at her junior high, and she sang the song "Hallelujah" (the version from the movie *Sing*). OMG, it gave me chills. It was like a divine message. That song just spoke to me so much when she sang it, and I was so grateful to get out of that toxic job.

I resigned on Friday, April 13, 2018, and immediately got back on unemployment. This time, I was determined to find a work-from-home gig that was NOT a management role. I was done with that level of stress. I didn't want to manage a team anymore. I was done working hard. I needed to work smart.

Then, I found out that my dad had bladder cancer. SIGH. It never stops, right?

Honestly, I believe that everything happens for a reason. If I had not quit my job at that time, I wouldn't have been able to be there when my dad was going through hospice because his bladder cancer diagnosis was at its end stage. The only option was to put him in hospice care so that he could pass peacefully. I'm so grateful that I left that job. And it was so weird because I was grateful that I was sick. What? It was my excuse to leave that job and the commute and to be with my dad. Not that I needed an excuse. I wish I had been strong enough in 2016 to insist on applying for disability then. But everything happens for a reason, and you can't change the past. It allowed me to be with my dad daily, to spend quality time with him at home, in hospice.

This was the summer of 2018. I had a follow-up with my GI and paid cash for my colonoscopy (I had to pay cash because I left my job and we didn't have insurance). I was officially diagnosed with acute ulcerative colitis. It broke me. When my GI came into the recovery room after my colonoscopy and told me that I had UC, I lost it. I was crying uncontrollably. I was so crushed. All I could think about was all the shit my dad went through while dealing with it. He got diagnosed with UC first, then prostate cancer, then colorectal cancer, and now he was at home in hospice care with bladder cancer. And now, I had ulcerative colitis, too. It was so difficult to tell my parents that. It was so sad.

I got back on unemployment and was interviewing for jobs. The UC was flaring ALL THE TIME! I was doubled over with cramps, had extreme diarrhea, and lost a lot of weight. I could barely eat anything at all. I cried every single day. The only peace I got was that I was at home. I was on so many antibiotics, trying to keep the gut biome to where it would stop being so inflamed. I had so many C diff infections. I was doubled over, cramping all day.

In the early morning of August 12, 2018, my sweet dad passed away. This sent the UC into a MASSIVE flare. I was stressed out because of my dad. Thankfully, I'd accepted an offer for a job and bought a brand-new AudiQ3 just days before he passed away, so I was able to share that good news with him. He got to see me be somewhat happy before he passed.

I was supposed to start my new job the following week. But I had to get through this week first! I was doubled over with severe cramps for three days straight. I had to go to the ER the night before my dad's funeral. As soon as the IV was started and the morphine hit, I finally felt relief for the first time in DAYS. I prayed they would just overdose me and be done with it. I was so sick of this shit. In truth, I kept looking at my dad's morphine while he was in hospice care; it was right there in front of me, but I was too scared to take it. And I didn't want to leave my family. I was afraid of death. Not yet.

They sent me home with more Bentyl and also Norco. My instructions said to take a dose every six hours. It was laughable. After the level of pain that I had endured my whole life, did they really think that taking a painkiller every six hours was going to help me? Bitch, please! I was taking it every three hours. It was the ONLY way I could function at all.

The saddest part about this is that I remember practically NOTHING from my dad's funeral. All I remember is rocking back and forth in the pew, hunched over, crying, cramping, dizzy, hovering between reality and death, feeling so overwhelmed with it all. I remember being jealous that my dad was no longer in pain, but I was still stuck here suffering. I WAS JEALOUS! I was begging God, Waheguru, anyone who would listen, *Please, please, please just let this be over. Just let this pain end. Please put me out of my misery. I really do not want to go through this. I do not want to be here. I don't want to do this anymore.* But I was also terrified of death and didn't want to leave my family. How could I leave them? What kind of monster was I?

CHAPTER 10

I'M USED TO THIS PAIN

A PAIN THAT I'M USED TO
Depeche Mode

What is the point of all of this pain?
I'm becoming harder to console.
I have lost complete control of my life.
Just give me more pain.
It's fine.
I'm used to it.

So, here's a quick recap on the timeline. My dad died on August 12. On August 14th, I was in the ER for horrific UC cramping. The next day was my dad's funeral. I don't remember anything from my dad's funeral. I was so drugged up, popping Norco like candy. I had to take it every three hours to stay upright. Imagine having contractions all fucking day long. No breaks. The memorial ceremony at Gurdwara was on August 17. I couldn't attend that final funeral ceremony because of my pain, cramping, and diarrhea. It was devastating not being able to be with my mom and siblings. I had to watch my own dad's funeral service on Facebook Live. I can't even explain in words what that did to me. It was so incredibly shitty.

My faith was in massive decline. I was questioning EVERYTHING. What the fuck was the point of any of it? Mind you, I wasn't super religious anyway, but all of this health drama and loss and back-to-back trauma? Why was this happening to me?

The following week, I started a new job. SHIT. I should not have been working at this time. PERIOD. I felt like I was DYING. I felt like no one was listening to me! I started that job on August 20. On the 21st, I had another UC flare. By the following month, I had stopped coloring my hair. This was a *HUUUUUUGE* decision for me. I have had gray hair since I was 18 or 19 years old and had been coloring my hair ever since then.

This was a massive deal because, for my whole life, the ONLY thing I could control was how I looked. That's it. Nothing else. And I put every effort into it. My hair, my face, it was ALL I had control over, so I made sure that I always looked good. My hair was always funky colors in the purple-red color range. I loved it and took so much pride in how I looked. I also went to the gym, worked out, and did A LOT of aqua aerobics. The pool was the best thing for me! This was everything to me. It was ALL I had. Until I stopped caring. I had zero fucks to give at that point. I was SOOOO done with life and unimportant things like vanity. I was so done with everything. The last time I went to the gym was sometime in 2015 because my health had been declining. Now, I was done keeping up my appearance completely. I gave up control. It was the LAST thing that belonged to me... and I let it go. I didn't care. I was struggling to survive, but I also didn't want to be here. I wanted it to be over. I wanted to be gone from this earth. It felt like rock bottom and I felt so bad that my husband and my child were witnessing all of this. I can't even imagine the toll it was taking on them! I was so angry with my circumstances.

Thankfully, the job that I had gotten was less pressure, a regular sales rep position, compared to being in management. I couldn't take any more stress, and I was NOT trying to be anybody's supervisor. I didn't even have the mental capacity to take care of myself, much less manage a team. So, I got a job as a rep, working from home as an account executive. Thankfully, I was well enough to go to Arizona for a three-day job training.

I was supposed to go for my official rookie training over the week of Halloween, but I had another massive UC flare, so I couldn't go. I was in the hospital for an ENTIRE week. During that week, I had another C diff infection. This was the very first hospital stay for me where my husband didn't stay with me overnight. He'd stayed overnight with me for every other hospital stay (four times). I was fine with it. He needed to be home with our daughter.

The UC got worse, and I was put on steroids, lovely steroids. Stupid fucking drug. This time, the steroids were meant to decrease the swelling in my colon, and the best way to do that is with a suppository. How do I put this? I have CHRONIC Rheumatoid Arthritis. I couldn't get down there to put the suppositories in because of the condition of my fingers, hands, wrists, elbows, and shoulders. I just didn't have the range of motion to be able to do it myself. So, I had to ask my husband to do it for me. Damn. Nothing will test your marriage as much as something like this.

It was embarrassing, humbling, and so incredibly sad to have to ask my husband to do that for me. I was at my most vulnerable point, and I just wanted my life to be over. How was it even possible for one human being to cry as much as I did during this time? I was at my lowest point. Or so I thought. And praying? But who was listening? Has anyone ever listened? I was in a downward spiral with no end in sight. Again, I did not want to be there. Right after that, my husband got me some marijuana for pain relief because I had to find some sort of solace somewhere. I started using it.

By November, I started feeling weird in my lungs. By December, I found out I had a mold in my lungs called aspergillosis. Why was it there? Probably from bad weed. REALLY? Unbelievable. At this point, I was starting to laugh at shit because I was not catching a break with ANYTHING. Seriously, maybe this was a sign? But what about all of the other shit I was going through? You have to laugh every once in a while, right? I felt like such a terrible mom and wife. I couldn't take care of my family anymore. Hell, I could barely take care of myself.

By January of 2019, the UC finally calmed down. The suppositories were helping a little bit. Some of the other things I was doing were helping, too. I was taking a very strong probiotic called Visbiome – six pills a day, every day. For the aspergillosis in my lungs, they put me on such a strong antibiotic that it was causing liver issues, so I had to get off of it. Then I went to an infectious disease doctor, and he determined that I didn't need to be on antibiotics for it and that it would clear up on its own because it wasn't so bad. So, I got that little bit of good news, and thankfully, the UC was at bay. *Was it too good to be true? Were things looking up just a little bit?* Yeah, for a minute. But then…

In February 2019, I had a massive RA flare. I don't know if it was because of my job. I was sitting in front of my laptop all day. It was a regular sales job, so you had to log in and be on your computer at your allotted time, 8 a.m. to 5 p.m., ALL DAY in one position. My right hand was killing me! I had to get a special mouse for my laptop that could accommodate my wrist because my right wrist was killing me. My right foot was killing me, too. The big toe on my right foot had collapsed. I can't even begin to tell you how excruciating that pain is. I started prednisone for the RA flare in addition to getting the steroid treatment suppository for the ulcerative colitis.

I was taking Humira for both the RA and the UC, as it was approved for both diseases. But I had to go on a different medication because, even though it's also good for ulcerative colitis, I had gone from taking it every two weeks for the RA alone to taking it weekly to deal with and take care of two different autoimmune diseases, the RA and the ulcerative colitis. But once I started taking it every week versus every two weeks, it was destroying my liver, so I had to explore other options. My GI and rheumatologist had a consultation. I needed another treatment for RA and another treatment for ulcerative colitis. When you change treatments that your body is already used to, especially when there is no reason for it other than liver issues, it is horrible for your body, but now I was switching my RA treatment to Orencia (self-injection) and my UC treatment to Entyvio (IV infusion).

At this point, I had around four to five doctor's appointments every single month. Everything was falling apart. I also found out that I was in the beginning stages of having cataracts, but I wasn't a candidate for surgery because of my "young" age. Lol. "Young." I also had a lung CT scan done because of all of the issues with the aspergillosis. Thankfully, that was going away. And guess what? I didn't have interstitial lung disease! *LOLOLOLOL.* Remember that story? So many years later, I finally found out. Then, a bone-density test revealed that I have osteopenia, the beginning stages of osteoporosis. Lovely, right? I got a cortisone shot in my right wrist, and my surgeon strongly advised me that I needed to have surgery to fuse that wrist before it self-fused. I'm right-handed. That's my dominant hand. I also started getting recurrent UTIs because of all of the antibiotic treatments I was on for the stupid C diff and other colon infections and the UC. And what's the treatment for a UTI? Yup, you guessed it: more antibiotics. It was like a fucking ouroboros, an endless cycle, going around and around and around in circles. Infection, antibiotics, infection, antibiotics. Never ending.

I started the new treatment for UC, Entyvio, which was an infusion. I had to go into a facility to have those done. That was ridiculous because they could never find my veins. I don't think I mentioned this before, but I've always been a hard stick. My veins are super tiny, and I was in the hospital so much during 2018! You should have seen what my arms looked like during that time! I was bruised beyond belief! I have pictures documenting the bruises. People probably thought I was a heroin addict. I was bruised all over my arms, from my hands all the way to my elbow and then up toward my shoulders. They could never find my veins, and they blew them constantly.

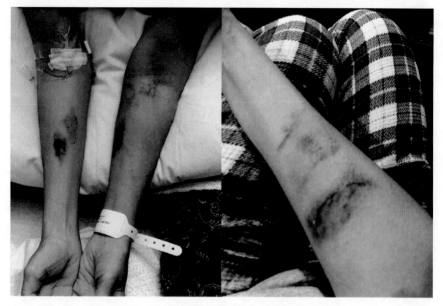

Painful bruising from IV. Fun fact: Arnica gel works VERY well to relieve the pain and the bruising. I didn't find that out until much later in my journey!

Plus, when you have severe diarrhea, it's very difficult to stay hydrated. I had lost so much weight during that time and was trying to drink as much water as I could. I had to go on a gluten-free diet. I couldn't even handle eating regular foods, and I had no fiber at all. No fruits or veggies. I survived on white bread, eggs, and chai that year.

It was unbelievable how much pain I was in during that time. When I was in the hospital over Halloween, I had pediatric and ER nurses trying to find my veins with ultrasound machines. And the veins would STILL blow out! It was awful and SO FUCKING painful! Have you ever had an IV started deep INSIDE your arm? That was my only option. And that blew, too! Oh, that was painful.

I had a surgery consultation to fix my right wrist, and I needed to have surgery on my right foot to fix my collapsed big toe. Seriously, somebody, please just shoot me! I needed to have the collapsed big toe fused. I didn't know how long I was going to last in this work environment, either. At this point, I was only six months into this job, but I knew my body was shutting down. I knew the time was coming for me to finally step down from all of it. However, the only way I could have the surgeries I needed was if insurance paid for them, so I was laser-focused on getting everything fixed that needed to be fixed before my body shut down.

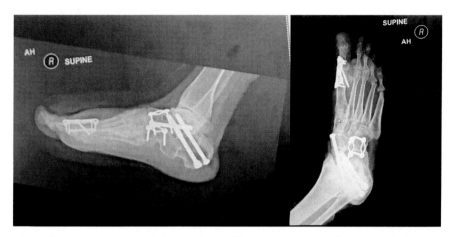

My right foot, post-op from the big toe fusion. The other hardware is from my ankle fusion: triple arthrodesis–first in 1998, second in 2009.

I had my right big toe fused first – a three-inch plate was put in, full fusion. I went back to work the following Monday. Let me clarify. I had the surgery on a Friday, and I couldn't take any time off. The only PTO day I got was Friday, the day of the surgery. It was a brand-new job. I was only six months into the position. I had to go back to work the following Monday. How the hell did I do it? It's a miracle I lasted. That whole week, I was in excruciating pain because I had to sit in front of the computer. All the blood was rushing down to my foot, and I couldn't elevate it as much as I needed to while I was working.

Then – and I'm not even exaggerating this – TWO WEEKS after I had my right toe fused, I went under AGAIN for my right wrist, a full fusion. This was a DOOZY. This pain was unlike any I had ever felt. I was in SO MUCH POST-OP PAIN that I BEGGED the anesthesiologist to give me a nerve block AFTER the surgery… in the recovery room! A nerve block is ONLY supposed to be administered prior to the procedure. But he did it for me because I was SCREAMING in pain! I was begging for relief.

I didn't realize how destroyed my wrist was until I saw the post-op X-rays. I noticed that the ulna joint in my right wrist was missing. My surgeon said, "Your ulna joint was in such bad shape that there was no way we could leave it inside of your body. It was a mush of debris. So many tiny broken shards." So, now I have a space there. It took a very long time for me to get used to seeing my hand like that. It was foreign and freaked me out. After the procedure, they bandaged me too tightly, and I was in a lot of post-op pain. I got something called blood blisters from the bandaging being too tight. Seriously? Apparently, that's a thing. It was ridiculous.

I had only gotten a nerve block once before during my shoulder replacement, and the long-term results were NOT good! I'm NOT a candidate for nerve blocks. My body does not like them. I went numb in my fingers for several months before the feeling returned after the shoulder replacement. Several MONTHS! Clearly, my body did not like nerve blocks, but post-op from this stupid wrist surgery, I was SO desperate for pain relief that I begged for one. I wish I had not gotten this nerve block now because it actually numbed my pinky and ring finger, and like before, I didn't regain the feeling back until several months later.

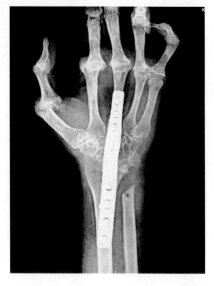

After the bandaging came off, I realized that something else was wrong with my wrist. Something was popping and moving inside, and it was painful, too! Turns out, because they cut out the ulna joint, the remainder of the bone that was left in my arm kept jumping up and

Post-op right wrist: Notice the missing ulna joint with a small hole where the surgeon re-tied the bone using a tendon. The collapsed thumb and broken MCP joints show failed implants from years ago.

144

down. This only happens in 10% of patients. LUCKY ME! Lol. It is very difficult to explain, but I'm going to try. Take your wrist and bend it: flex, extend, flex, extend. Near that ulna joint, there's a tendon that allows your wrist to move and make that motion. If the joint is removed, the bone has nothing to hold on to. The bone was bouncing up and down in my arm and causing a tremendous amount of pain. So, guess what the doctor had to do? DING, DING, DING, DING, DING. He had to go back in and do more surgery to tie down that bone using my tendon. That made three back-to-back surgeries.

At this point, I was already on short-term disability. It was VERY short term because I had only been at my new job for seven months now. By the time that third procedure rolled around, I realized I was done. I was going to recover for a bit and then apply for disability. I would not be able to go back to this job.

I had to get a cortisone shot in my left shoulder because it was starting to fall apart. I was told by that surgeon that I was losing time and that there might come a day when even a reverse total shoulder surgery would not be an option for me. My X-rays were not looking good. The left shoulder was just as bad as the right shoulder. Oh, and did I mention that my knuckles were all broken, too? The ones I had replaced back in 2003 and 2004? Granted, they'd been broken for several years, but now they were broken, swollen, in pain, and needed to be re-replaced soon. They were in REALLY bad shape. I was just getting bad news after bad news at this point.

A very good friend reached out and asked if I wanted a reiki session, and I said, "Sure, why not?" The session was really cool. She shared with me that she felt a very strong white light and presence around me as if my spiritual team were there and ready to help. I had never experienced anything like that. Keep in mind that my spirituality was non-existent at this time. I did not have any faith that my situation would ever improve. I felt like this was my new normal, but I couldn't help but ask why. What had I done to deserve all of these things that were happening to me? She gave me a glimmer of hope. Whoa! I hadn't experienced HOPE in forever!

That September, we went on a family trip to San Francisco so my husband and daughter could see Metallica play with the San Francisco Symphony. I stayed back with my cousin and hit up a medical marijuana dispensary. For the first time in a while, I had a real joint because I was terrified of smoking after the aspergillosis scare. It was a place called Moe Greens Dispensary and Lounge. It was magical! The budtender hooked me up with a smooth Indica strain from the Himalayan region of India. I felt so good when I walked out of there. It was the FIRST time in YEARS I did not have to take a painkiller and muscle relaxer at night.

Every night from about 2006, when I had my daughter, I would go to bed with a muscle relaxer and a painkiller. This was my nightly routine. If I forgot it, I would suffer for it. I DID THIS EVERY SINGLE NIGHT FOR YEARS! And this was the first time I did not take a muscle relaxer or a painkiller because I didn't feel that I needed it. I was feeling SO GOOD and so pain-free. How was that even possible? I only had a half of a joint. Keep this moment in the back of your mind because now that I'd had this experience, I was aware that there was something out there that could actually help me.

That happened on the last night of our trip. Prior to that, I had a VERY difficult time walking on this trip. We went to the Redwood Forest, and I sat in the visitor's center, miserable, while my family enjoyed the trails and gorgeous trees. I sat in Alcatraz while my family enjoyed the tour. I couldn't do shit. I couldn't enjoy anything. The most important moment during that trip for me was the marijuana and my pain relief.

Then my hips started to hurt, especially my left hip. I got cortisone shots in both hips. When I got them X-rayed, the surgeon said, "You actually don't have rheumatoid arthritis in your hips. You have bursitis."

I was like, "Really? What are the odds of that?" All this time, I thought I had RA in my hips, and I didn't, which probably explains the fact that I was able to give birth vaginally. Unbelievable. Was that a win? Hell, fucking yeah, it was! I'll take it.

Then, I had issues with my knees. *NOOOOOOOOOOOO!* Now, mind you, I hadn't had issues with my knees in DECADES since I'd gotten them replaced in 1994. But now they were buckling under me. I felt like my knee was slipping and I was going to fall. Something was definitely wrong. I think I noticed several years prior to this that I was having issues with my knees, but they just had to take a backseat, you know? My plate was fucking full! I didn't have time.

I finally went and had a consultation. Both knees were X-rayed. Honestly, I dropped the ball on this. After knee replacements, you're supposed to have them X-rayed every two to three years to stay on top of things. I couldn't remember the last time I'd had them X-rayed. I was too busy dying. Lol. My surgeon was not happy with the X-rays and ordered an MRI of both knees. He told me my implants were failing. SILENCE. I started tearing up. I was so overwhelmed. I felt so incredibly alone.

I went to this appointment by myself. There used to be a time when I would ask my husband to go to important doctor's appointments with me, but at some point, all that stopped. It was all too much. It was taking a toll on both of us, and it was definitely taking a toll on our marriage.

My left knee was in worse shape than the right. That implant had completely failed. Could it get any worse? Sadly, yes. He told me that the

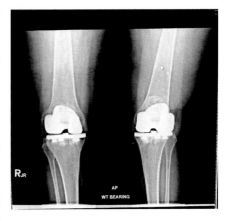

Failed implants - no more "cartilage" or space in between the parts. Left knee is clearly worse than the right knee.

plastic part of the implant, which is essentially the "cartilage" in the joint, had completely deteriorated, and now the two pieces of metal that constituted my joint were rubbing against each other without a barrier. So, unlike a regular joint that'll just break up and become shards of bone, the metal was being compromised. Uh, what? What did that even mean? Well, there was a slight possibility that I might have metal ion poisoning in my body. WHAT? Then I thought, *I wonder if that's what's causing all of the current issues with the UC and massive RA flares. Maybe it's because I have this metal ion poisoning in my body.* Honestly, you cannot make this shit up. It was insane. SO MUCH BAD NEWS. Back-to-back nonsense.

By this time, I'd already fallen apart, and I realized that my marriage was being challenged. I also got diagnosed with chronic dry eye disease. I finally started getting the feeling back in my fingers, though, the pinky and the ring finger that had been falling asleep after the nerve block I'd gotten post-surgery for my wrist. This was roughly in early November, and I'd had that procedure back in JUNE. That's how long it took for the feeling to return.

Buckle up! If you thought everything leading up to this point would have destroyed me a hundred times over, you're absolutely right. At this point, I was shocked that I'd survived as long as I had. But NOTHING, and I mean NOTHING, could have remotely prepared me for what was about to happen next.

CHAPTER 11

LEAVE ME IN SILENCE

LEAVE IN SILENCE
Depeche Mode

This song is OG Depeche Mode from their second album A Broken Frame.
I had reached a full stop at this point in my life.
My life was about to drop drastically.
We had reached our natural conclusion.
No more illusions.
There was no way to save this.
It was spreading like cancer.
Just go.
And leave me in silence.

On November 11, my husband went to a conference. In my mind we were fine. We loved each other, pure and simple, and everyone around us knew it and witnessed it.

On the 13th, I sat down in front of our Mac and started crying. I was filling out the disability application. It took me three to four hours, and I cried the entire time. In my brain, I was back in my doctor's office, sitting in a wheelchair, begging him to write me a prescription for a wheelchair, an actual wheelchair, and he was telling me, "Just give up! Just go get yourself an electric wheelchair. Get on disability and get on with your life." So, it took me back to a painful point, and I was like, *Fuck, I have to go back on disability again. What am I going to do? How am I going to do this?*

My husband came back home on the 15th. He was not the same person. The affection had COMPLETELY stopped. NOTHING. He was treating me like a stranger now, and I thought, *Whoa, what the fuck just happened? Is it because I applied for disability?* Don't get me wrong. He worked during our entire marriage, but I made more money for the vast majority of our time together. I truly felt as though he was doing this because of the disability. Today I know that was not the case, but that's what I thought at the time. He *knew* I had to apply. I simply could not work anymore.

The next day was my birthday, and he was still treating me without any affection. Keep in mind that my husband and I were VERY affectionate with one another, always touching, goofing off, laughing, kissing, hugging, sitting together, and just being playful both in private and in public. And yes, while our relationship had fallen apart during the last five to six years, the affection had never stopped completely. Never. And when I say it stopped completely, it stopped COMPLETELY. There was zero affection. None whatsoever.

He took me to brunch on my birthday, and we barely spoke over our meal. Then, we went to our daughter's theater performance and picked up fast food and ice cream for dinner. Not much conversation. We were going to "celebrate" my birthday with the three of us going to my favorite ramen place the following day. Barely any conversation, and I teared up. I didn't know what was happening. Things were already shit, right?

When we got home, I confronted him. "What the hell is wrong with you? Did you cheat on me while you were at this conference?" (He didn't.) "Like, what is going on? You're treating me like we're not married. What's happening?"

With a strained face, he said, "I just feel like we don't love each other anymore."

It was so sad, but all I could think was, "What? Now? You're choosing to do this NOW?" Let me be clear: I KNEW my marriage was in a downward spiral. I simply didn't have time to think about it while dealing with everything else. But then I thought about *what* he said: "WE" don't love each other anymore. Don't tell me how I feel about you! Ask me! I loved him plenty! I broke into a million pieces. I was just completely blown away. My brain blew up. There's no other way to describe how it felt, like the most vivid nightmare I'd ever had. I was dumbfounded, shocked, and COMPLETELY blindsided. Was he even living in the same house as me? Was this the man that I married? How DARE YOU! Do you not see me? And the SHIT that I'm going through right now? Do you not care? Dude, I JUST applied for disability. I JUST signed everything away and gave up my career. And now THIS? I feel like I'm succumbing to all this bullshit health crap, and this is your timing? This is what you're coming to me with? You said WE don't love each other anymore. You also said that we probably need marriage counseling. I was totally on board with that part. Let's go! Let's do it. Lord knows I NEED it so much right now. Oh, God.

I felt so crushed. What about my baby? She was only 13. He wasn't the same man. He withheld affection and only barely greeted me all day. I got a few hugs that felt like pity hugs. All major affection had ceased at this point. The man that I'd married and had been with for the last 19 years was gone. I didn't know if this marriage was sustainable. Based on the way he was treating me, I didn't want him anyway.

He disrespected me and our vows. He removed his wedding and engagement rings, and when I asked him why, knowing that we were going to go to therapy and try to fix it, his response was, "It's just pageantry." What the hell? Our rings were just pageantry to him? This man asked my dad for my hand in marriage. My dad was VERY clear with him about my many health issues and that there might come a day when I could no longer work.

He told my dad that he'd always take really good care of me for our entire lives, no matter what. We took vows in both a regular courthouse and a traditional Sikh wedding. *"In sickness and in health."* And he loved me so much. He DID. This is important because he really did love me and took such good care of me. I was very grateful to have such a doting husband. But where had he gone? This man was *not* him. It was like there was a timeline switch, and another person, a complete stranger, was sharing our space.

I was so grateful that my dad passed and wouldn't have to see me like this. But I had to consider my elderly mom. My siblings decided not to share the marital drama with her unless the marriage was seriously over. My husband and I also kept everything as quiet as possible for our child, but she was 13 and smart enough to observe that we were "off" and that he was not the same happy-go-lucky dad.

I started looking into therapy for us and soon found a therapist for him and one for myself. The plan was to do therapy individually first and then go to couples therapy. Then I started to get numbness in my feet. I'd never had this issue before. It just started happening. It was all too much. I thought about killing myself. My daughter loved her dad so much. She'd always had a closer relationship with him because she spent more time playing with him than me. Even though I worked from home, I traveled a lot and was exhausted by the time I got home. He took such great care of her and was an amazing father to her. I knew she'd be fine without me. Everyone would be just fine without me.

We had a gun cabinet at home. I opened it and stared at the gun. The only thing that was going through my head was: *My hands aren't even strong enough to hold the gun, much less pull the trigger.* On top of that, I didn't want to misfire. If I was going to shoot myself, I needed it to be OVER. I didn't want to be left in a vegetative state. I wanted a guarantee that it would be over because I was done with this world. I cried for almost an hour, like I'd never cried before. I had no idea I could cry as much as I did at that moment. Just sobbing. Shit, I'd been crying my whole life, but this cry really broke me. This was rock bottom.

When I finally regained my composure, I felt SO guilty for doing it, not because of him but because of my child. How dare I even think about abandoning my child like that? After everything I'd gone through to HAVE her? To even get pregnant? NO. NO. I had to think about my child and how this might affect us.

I made an appointment with a neurologist to find out what was going on with this numbness on the soles of my feet, and my husband and I started therapy. We had separate therapists. When I say the floodgates opened during my very first session, I'm not exaggerating. My poor therapist! I CRIED for the entire hour, sobbing as I tried my best to tell her about ALL of the trauma I had endured my whole life! It came out as a bumbling mess. This story makes me laugh today because I think I scared the shit out of her with my uncontrollable sobbing. OMG. Poor lady! She referred me to a psychiatrist because I was having major panic attacks and wanted to unalive myself.

And my husband? I begged him for affection. Through tears streaming down my face, I BEGGED this man standing in front of me to forgive me for anything that I had done wrong throughout our entire marriage. I begged him to hold me. Nothing I said made a difference. Nothing. When your spouse sees you having a panic attack, and they finally hold you because you're begging for affection, without ANY compassion or love in the embrace, it's utterly defeating. This wasn't the man I married. This guy, I did not *like* at all, much less love.

I was diagnosed with panic disorder, anxiety disorder, and severe depression with suicidal tendencies and put on two different antidepressants. Christmas was right around the corner. Should I shop for him? What were the rules? We were still in individual therapy. We were trying to act as "normal" as possible around our daughter because we didn't want to upset her too much, but she knew we were having marital issues. On Christmas Day, we opened presents, and everything seemed to be okay. Heck, we were going to start couples therapy soon, right? That night we had a conversation where he shared that he didn't think joint counseling would help us. The day after Christmas Day, we had a conversation in the morning about what he said the night before.

I wasn't sure what he was trying to say the night before and wanted clarification.

I asked him point blank, "so, you don't want to go to counseling together?" His response was, "Nope." After all these years together? NOPE? My heart started racing and I started shaking. I was *fired up*. I was so fucking pissed. I said, "Well, if you don't want to do counseling, then there isn't any other option other than a divorce. Is that what you want?"

He said, "YEP." THAT was his response. Already disrespected, I told him that he would be the one to tell our daughter. Let him share *his decision* to end this without trying to salvage it. Even though I didn't like this version of him, I was still in love with the man I married and was TOTALLY on board with couples therapy and to at least try to make an attempt at salvaging our marriage.

I wanted him to be the one to tell our daughter so that she knew this was NOT my decision. I wanted her to hear from his lips what he wanted for his future. He sat down at the table next to her during breakfast. I came out of the room and sat on the other side of her, and he told her.

The first thing our child said to him, through tears streaming down her face, was, "What about Mommy? Who's going to take care of Mommy? She can't work anymore." I was GUTTED, but I was also so incredibly angry. SO FUCKING ANGRY. A light bulb switched on in my head when my child said that.

I immediately got up, crying – not for myself but for her. She LOVED her dad so much! This news *crushed* her. I hugged her and said, "That is not your problem, baby. As your mother, it is MY responsibility to take care of you. You and me. We are going to be good. We're going to be okay. I promise. I will do whatever it takes. We are going to be okay." I had already told him that our daughter was going to live with me. I wouldn't contest anything else in the divorce and just wanted to get it over with.

Have you ever felt anguish? True anguish? Never before had I felt that level of anguish. What was I thinking? How was I going to do this all by

myself? Shit, I was on my deathbed. I DIDN'T EVEN KNOW IF I WOULD
BE APPROVED FOR DISABILITY YET. You don't get notified that quickly.
I was so lost and so alone. I honestly didn't know what to do or how I would
take care of myself and my child. But I didn't care. My child needed me, and
that was all the ammunition I needed.

I couldn't stand to see him. He would go out and stay out all night, not
coming home until the next day. It was so immature and stupid to do that in
front of his child, not to mention disrespectful to me, so I asked him to leave
us and go elsewhere. I didn't care where. He went to his brothers.

Later that night, I was sitting on the couch with my daughter, watching
a show. All of a sudden, my right arm went completely numb. COMPLETELY
NUMB. The first thing I thought was, *Oh, shit, I'm having a heart attack.* But
then I thought, *Wait a second. I think that's the left arm, not the right arm.* Lol.
Gotta find the funny, right? Again, it's funny as hell today, but back then, it
was not humorous at all.

Then, a burning sensation engulfed my arm. It felt like it was on fire. I
FREAKED out. I was at home alone with my 13-year-old. I took every single
pain medication I had on hand. Keep in mind that I always kept my leftover
pain medications every time I had surgery, so I had a full arsenal at my
disposal. I took everything I had, but nothing was helping. The pain gradually
became so excruciating that it was unbearable. Imagine your arm falling
asleep – the whole arm, from shoulder to fingertips – and then THROBBING
with pain like it's on fire. It was awful.

I finally buckled.

At 3 a.m., I called my husband and said, "I'm sorry for calling you late. I
know you're probably asleep."

"Hey," he said. "What's up?"

"I just had something happen," I told him, "and I need to go to the ER."

"Oh, do you need me to take you?"

"No, just come home to be with our child. I'll take myself to the
emergency room."

I was hopped up on so many painkillers that I honestly don't know how I made it to the ER. I had been taking them every two hours, hoping for some sort of relief, something that would work for me, but nothing did. They started an IV and gave me morphine. It kicked in immediately and quieted all of the throbbing pain and fire. Then they did a bunch of scans and told me that, most likely, I had peripheral neuropathy and needed to follow up with a neurologist.

"Well," I said, "my feet have started going numb, too, so I figured that was who I'd be following up with. I've got that appointment coming up anyway. Please, God, no more diagnoses. Stop."

The ER wouldn't let me drive back home on my own. I told them I had no other choice and begged them to let me go. It was just down the street. Why? They had me on Oxy and didn't want me driving. I told them, "This is my life. I made it here, and I'll make it back home. Please let me go." And they did. This diagnosis was due to the stress from my disability situation and the divorce, no doubt about it. I was fed up, absolutely fed up and sick of it.

That following January, I started steroid infusions for chronic nerve pain. I went in for IV steroids for an entire week! It didn't do anything for my nerve pain. I was taking Gabapentin and then Lyrica, trying to do anything to help myself. I had to keep ice packs on that arm to keep the fire at bay. Ironically, during this time, my husband had a two-week work trip in India. While he was there, I had a clear mind, and something clicked. On February 1, 2020, something happened. No, not COVID, but it was coming. Something switched in my brain. I woke up that morning feeling like that was the true beginning of my awakening. As I'm writing this, I'm looking at the clock, and it says "5:55," so that's my confirmation.

I woke up and I was like, fuck this shit. That little voice inside my head came out with a vengeance. She was *MAAAAAAAAAAD*. *Do you honestly think you went through ALL of this shit in life simply to sit back and give up like this? FUCK NO! Since when? We don't go out like that. We've NEVER gone out like that. We did not suffer for years for it to end like this. No Ma'am. So*

156

pull up your GODDAMN britches, stop your fucking whining and take care of your child! And While you're at it, figure your own shit out, turn your life around and STOP with this victim mode shit. YOU are NOT a victim. Look at YOU! Look at how far you have come. YOU ARE A SURVIVOR (yes, Queen Bee, I AM!), so STOP THIS NONSENSE and CHANGE YOUR REALITY! Make it happen.

I kid you not; I packed up the majority of our house while my husband was in India. I put Post-it notes on every box and piece of furniture, labeling what was mine and what was his. I was like, if you want a divorce, I am happy to give you a divorce, but it will be on *my terms.* How I got the strength to pack, I don't know. But I recognized this Jasmine! She had been dormant for YEARS. This version of me was emerging from the fire. I felt like a fucking PHOENIX... rising from the ashes. The adrenaline running through my broken body at this time was unbelievable. I PACKED UP EVERYTHING.

Then I asked my sweet spiritual friend to come over, and we smudged the house. She said there was a very weird energy in that house, which made sense, given that we'd had A LOT of bad luck in that house. I believe in shit like that. Now, I started thinking about energy, especially my own. This happened at the beginning of 2020. COVID was happening, and the entire world was shutting down. I'd also still received no word from disability. My husband and I decided to wait until the disability decision to officially file for divorce.

Now, remember how my knee replacements were failing? Well, by this time, I had the results from the scans and procedure they'd done. And it's funny because, well, not funny, funny, but funny. It's just funny, whatever. You HAVE to find the humor in situations. I had a procedure done where they insert a scope into your knee and suction out the liquid. My knees were getting really swollen, but it was due to the implant failing. When the surgery tech started extracting what was inside my knee, he said, "Whoa."

"What?" I asked. "Why'd you say that, homie?" I was like, you can't do that, dude. You can't say "whoa" when you're working on my knee. "What is it that you see?"

"I'm not supposed to say anything."

"Please, tell me what the hell you're talking about."

"I've never seen an extraction this dark, and it's coming out of your knee." He showed me, and it was practically black. Clearly, I had metal ions floating around in that knee, but was it affecting all this other shit that was happening to me? I knew that I had to get my knees replaced again anyway.

My old, faithful surgeon from 1994, who had evolved into a loving father figure for me, had retired. I found the best surgeon in Houston and booked an appointment with him. I made it very clear to his staff while booking the appointment that this would be a case unlike any other, given my age. I was 49 and about to have my knees re-replaced! The first set of knees had lasted 26 years! That's amazing. In 1994, they told me that knee replacements could last a lifetime based on wear and tear. Realistically, the life expectancy for a knee implant was ten years, so I was incredibly grateful that mine lasted for so long!

When the surgeon saw me for the first time, he was shocked at the condition of my knees, but he also applauded me for my strength after hearing my medical and surgical history. He was floored. No word from disability yet.

On March 17, 2020, St Patrick's Day, I had a revision total knee replacement for my left knee. I didn't know it at the time, but my surgery was the very last before they shut the hospital down due to COVID-19. This was a scary time, especially with my shitty immune system.

Remember how I said that I had gotten a whole week's worth of IV steroids that didn't work for the excruciating nerve pain earlier this year? While I was getting the steroid infusions for the neuropathy, I met this beautiful soul who was sitting in a chair next to me, having infusions for her debilitating MS. She told me how marijuana had saved her life, and she gave me some "flower" in a container to try for myself. She said that marijuana had really helped her with her pain, swelling, and ability to function. I'm certain she felt sorry for me. I was in PEAK victim mode. This was before I had my "not today, Satan" moment on February 1.

All this time, I was looking into medical marijuana and what my options were in Texas. There was nothing in Texas at the time. Fast forward to the first knee revision. I got my first cart and started using it. It was helping – a lot. My surgeon also encouraged me to get a pain management doctor before the surgery so I could get some serious pain meds. It was my first time being prescribed the drug Nucynta, and I needed it for post-op and recovery.

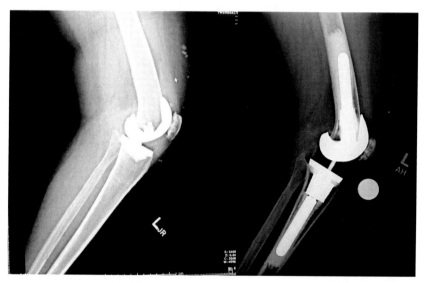

OG left knee from 1994 on the left and my beautiful brand new left knee on the right!!!

Check out the before and after X-rays of my left knee. Now, I had a shiny metal rod in the marrow of my leg. This was painful, but I am a warrior. Always have been and always will be. Badass Jasmine was slowly starting to re-emerge, and during COVID, no less! Lol. I should have been *soooooo* terrified of getting sick, but I wasn't. Do you know why? Because, for the first time in my life, I had no fear. All these years, my greatest fear had been dying, but now I wasn't afraid of it anymore. It was so empowering.

I was diligent with my PT, and my physical therapist was astonished by my fast recovery. Y'all, amidst all of this nonsense, the divorce, my unknown disability status, and COVID, I was actually happy. For the first time in YEARS! I didn't even let it phase me when I was denied disability! I know. How the fuck was I DENIED? With my extensive history? I'm the poster child for "disabled." That's kind of funny. Lol. Basically, I was warned in advance that EVERYONE is denied the first time. It's a business, right? They need to give business to the law firms fighting for our rights. It's sad. This world is so corrupt. But I digress. I reached out to a wonderful law firm, which helped with my claim, and within weeks of reapplying, it was approved. HUZZAH!!!! I got a WIN! A REALLY BIG WIN! The monthly amount wasn't going to be anywhere near my old six-figure salary, but it was something, and I could work with that.

By early June, they reopened hospitals, and I got clearance to have my right knee redone on June 8, 2020. I was prioritized for surgery, given my circumstances. While I was approved for disability, I wouldn't qualify for or be eligible for Medicare until January 2021. Currently, I was on my husband's insurance, but we were getting a divorce.

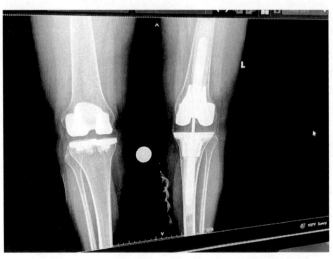

Post op - brand new knees–2020 version! Look at all of
that glorious space between the joints!

The fear came back. I had so many doctors, surgeons, appointments, and diagnoses. How the hell was I going to do this? All I knew for certain was that I wanted the divorce to happen and to move on with my life.

COVID was rampant, we were sanitizing everything, I'd had both knees replaced and was going through PT for both of them, and the clock was ticking as to how long I'd have insurance as a spouse. I'm not going to sugarcoat it; it was very stressful. But I was still happier than I'd ever been. I even added a cute pink to my graying hair to liven things up a bit. I was starting to look good! I got a new, funky nose ring and started taking care of my appearance again for the first time since 2015! My knees already looked tremendously better than before surgery. Now, I was starting to see a transformation. My legs were becoming more shapely. What? I didn't even know that was possible.

Our divorce was final on August 13, 2020. For perspective, during my 20 years with my ex, I had seven different diagnoses, most of them chronic, and 23 surgeries. 23!!! I know it was a lot. I know it was overwhelming for him as my husband and caretaker. I know it was challenging. And I KNOW that I was so mad about my circumstances and took it out on everyone around me, but I didn't deserve to be abandoned the way I was. I didn't deserve to be treated so callously. I shed a few tears on the day our divorce was finalized, but I was ready to move on. I also knew that it HAD to happen like this. I 100% believe this! If it had not happened like this, EXACTLY like this, I would not be the person I am today. I must repeat that. I WOULD NOT BE THE PERSON I AM TODAY! For that, I am incredibly grateful!

And I knew that I needed to get my shit together. I needed to get on with my life. I realized that I had something to live for now: myself AND my baby girl. We were going to be okay. I had already been approved for disability, my knees were healing VERY well, and my legs were starting to get their shape back. I have to add how much of a relief I felt throughout my body when I found out I was approved. I cried like a baby that this was the *second* time in my life that I'd been forced to take this route, but at the same time, I felt so overwhelmingly relieved that I could finally stop, sit down, relax, be with my child, and finally heal, finally LISTEN to my body.

Once the stress of having to work disappeared, my body was thrilled. And that, my friends, was the birth of my spiritual awakening. That was the aha moment that I needed to do whatever it took to NEVER let this happen again and reinforced my Never Give Up mantra!

CHAPTER 12

PHOENIX RISING

ENJOY THE SILENCE
Depeche Mode

Finally, it was over.
I was free.
And everything I ever wanted or needed
Was right here.
In my arms.
Silence.

Another song comes to mind here, "True Faith" by New Order. The lyrics never resonated so much for me as they did at this particular point in my life.

TRUE FAITH
New Order

I never thought this day would ever come!
I actually felt happiness seeing the sun.
The sun was like a drug taking me back to my lost childhood.
I was overcome with fear for so long.
I had forgotten how happy I felt in the sun!

And lastly, phoenix motherfucking rising! This is my comeback, bitches, and this time, it's personal! It's an apology to myself for putting up with so much shit that I did not deserve.

FIREBORN
Derivakat

I LOVE this song so much!
My daughter introduced this song to me from her Minecraft playing days.
The lyrics resonated with every single fiber of my being!
I was surviving, like a phoenix on repeat.
NO ONE was ever going to burn me again.
I was born in fire.
I have been rising from the ashes my whole life!
So go ahead and light it up.
I'm FIREBORN baby!

FINALLY! I was back! The nosedive "Into the Abyss" (shoutout to Rezz) was over! I felt like I was bungee jumping into a dark cave with a broken bungee. Right before hitting the bottom, that bungee cord snapped and almost dropped me, but then it bounced me right out. It was like my spiritual team collectively said, "Psych! You're not going out like that, and this is absolutely NOT the end of your story. This is not the way things are going to end with you, sister, so buckle up and get ready to do some serious work!"

I was ready. I was done being in pain. I was done being depressed. I was done trying to control things that I had zero control over. I finally let that shit go. The biggest thing about control is that I finally realized that the only thing in this world that I have full control over is myself – nothing and nobody else. Once you come to that realization, it is such a profound "come to Jesus" moment! LET THAT SHIT GO! For once, I had a clear perspective and was ready to start my official healing journey. I let it all go and said to God, Babaji, Waheguru, and the Universe, "Take the wheel because I am done steering." I completely changed and finally asked for spiritual help and guidance for me and my child.

Quick recap: February 1, 2020, was "that" absolute "aha" moment for me. It was like a load was lifted off my chest. I could finally breathe! Then, my disability was approved. More weight was lifted off my chest. The divorce was finalized on August 13, one day after the anniversary of my dad's passing. I knew about the date when it was set, but I didn't care. I just wanted to get it over with and move on. SO MUCH weight lifted. Thankfully, my ex offered to keep me on his insurance with approval from his HR department so I would at least have medical coverage until I could qualify for Medicare in January 2021. I WAS SO GRATEFUL!

On August 14, I filed all the paperwork to legally change my name back to my maiden name. Then, on August 30, 2020, it was moving day for me and my daughter! OMG! I was so excited and elated! Two single girls on the loose, baby! Lol. We actually said that while we were out shopping one day. This was so difficult for her, too. God, it was killing me to see her go through this. All she ever knew was two parents who adored each other, and for her to witness our downfall during her own middle school turmoil was gut-wrenching. I vowed to do everything in my power to make her happy. It started with her seeing me focus on myself for once and actually making myself better rather than being a victim and dependent on others. It made me sick to think that my daughter had witnessed her strong, badass mom fall apart at the seams. I had to make up for it. For me and for her!

I had been exploring marijuana use for the RA and everything else I had, and I began to notice benefits like pain relief and less inflammation. So, I decided to use it more consistently and see if, maybe, just maybe, I might be able to get off of at least one of the 15-plus pharmaceutical prescription meds I was currently consuming. The first ones I stopped taking were the two antidepressants. Another win!

As soon as my daughter and I moved out, I started reconnecting with people I felt like I had pushed away. Remember, I had been nosediving into that deep, dark cave for YEARS! I'd pushed everyone away: friends, family members, cousins, everyone. So, I started reaching out to people that I hadn't spoken to in years, some since 2016 when I went into this depression. I reconnected with my cousins, too. Two of my immediate cousins are middle children like me, and all three of us are the black sheep in our families – lol. We have a special connection.

I started spending more time with my siblings and my mom, but there was a problem: My mom didn't know about my divorce. I still hadn't told her. It was KILLING me to lie to her, but my siblings insisted that it would be best given her health and age. She always worried about me and my health and being with someone who could take care of me. This news would have killed her. I know it wasn't the greatest choice at the time, but I didn't want to do anything to jeopardize my mom's health.

Remember, she'd just lost my dad the year before. I didn't want her freaking out, wondering, "Who is going to take care of Rosy? How is Rosy going to survive without a husband? How is Rosy going to do anything?" She knew what my condition was, and I didn't want to put her through that, so I didn't tell her. UGH. It was so brutal to lie. The holidays were the worst because she couldn't understand why he wasn't there. COVID was a great excuse, but how long would I be able to use that excuse?

One of the biggest parts of my healing journey was forgiving my ex. I was with this man for 20 years of my life, and the marriage overall was wonderful. It really was. He loved me so much, and I loved him so very much. We just grew apart. But it was critical to my journey and to me, my soul, and my body to forgive him. I want to officially let it all go – not to forget it, because I feel that we need to remember. You can't forget things like that because then you won't learn your lesson; you're not going to remember the mistakes that were made and steer clear of making the same ones later. You should be able to take that knowledge into the next relationship and find your bliss.

But I needed to forgive him. This was absolutely instrumental in my healing recovery. I requested we meet. We actually got together in person to have this conversation, a post-mortem, if you will, on our marriage. I know it sounds bizarre, but I'm telling you, if your relationship ends, it doesn't matter whether it's a marriage, a relationship, or a friendship in general; just have a post-mortem if you can. Get together with that individual. Tell them how you feel. Tell them what's going on in your head. Talk about your feelings, and if you get something back, great. If you don't, that's great, too. Just let it go. Let it go. Just release them with love, peace, and forgiveness, and let them go. It was the best decision I ever made. We had a wonderful, healing conversation and shared things we had never shared before and put ourselves in each other's shoes. At that moment, we knew that we would co-parent our child like the grown-ass adults that we are. And as I've said a million times, he's a good father to our child. That's all that matters. Due to COVID, my daughter was at home for her freshman year of high school. She spent two weeks with me and one week with her dad, and it worked for us.

My 50th birthday came and went. I treated myself to a hair appointment, where I asked my hairdresser and friend to make all of my hair even-toned, all gray. We needed several sessions to make this happen. This was the first one. She gradually started removing all of the old colors from my hair – the reds and pinks that were left over.

The holidays were also approaching. That was weird because we always spent Thanksgiving with my ex's family and Christmas with mine. In 2020, I spent my very first Thanksgiving alone because I didn't want my daughter to miss out on being with his side of the family. I was fine being alone, though it was the first time in 20 years. It was so surreal. I was completely by myself, and I handled it like a BOSS! I bought a catered meal and had a delicious apple pie for dessert, along with a good movie, and I was set! Overall, things were starting to move in a beautiful, positive way, and it was just a wonderful opportunity for me to be in this independent space with my child and for both of us to bond with one another.

For Christmas 2020, I decided to surprise my daughter with a trip to Kansas City to visit her best friend, whom she hadn't seen in a while due to COVID. I did this for two reasons. First, we all know what happened the previous Christmas with the divorce talk, and I was NOT about to sit back and watch my kid be sad and recall those awful memories. I wanted to create new, meaningful memories to replace the shit. Second, I didn't want to see my family on Christmas and have to dodge my mom's questions about my ex. So, it was a total surprise trip. My good friend and I planned it secretly and executed it perfectly! It was such a beautiful, magical trip! We had so much fun exploring KC and all of the gorgeous Christmas decorations and enjoying blissful peace. Funny story about this friend of mine too! She is the one who told me that if I ever write a book about my story, it should be titled, "How Depeche Mode Saved My Life." LOL. Go figure! Thank you, friend!

Around this time, my good friend and spiritual advisor introduced me to one of her friends because she thought he and I would get along well. We had both been dealt a shitty hand of cards in our lives, and he wanted to start a podcast and was looking for a partner. We had a conversation while I was in Kansas City and totally hit it off. We decided to start a podcast based on psychology. He's obsessed with it, and I have a degree in it. Lol. It's called *Unfiltered Mental Health Podcast,* and it's pretty much just fun and for edutainment purposes only, as neither of us is a professional in the psychological realm. BUT both of us love psychology, and we get along fabulously! Fun fact: We've actually never met in person before, and he's 30 years younger than me. We just totally mesh and have the same humorous and fun view of psychology.

All this was going down in late 2020. In January 2021, I had my very first surgery completely on my own and under my ex's insurance. I needed to have a procedure called an ostectomy, an excision of the fifth metatarsal head on three small toes on my left foot. The recovery and getting around was challenging, but I did it, managing the stairs in my apartment unit with help from my daughter. I also survived the brutal ice storm and freeze in Houston that turned our apartment into a 19-degree ice box! It was *SOOOOOOO* cold!

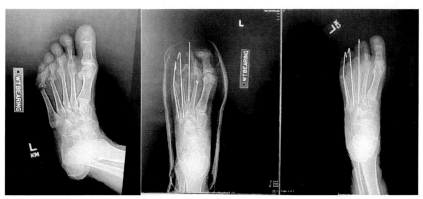

Left foot, pre-op on the left and post op on the right. The pins come out after 8 weeks. I still have them.

It wasn't until April 2021 that I finally got an opportunity to spill the beans to my mom. A window of opportunity emerged while we were chatting. She pulled me aside in the kitchen and said, "Rosy, tell me the truth. What's going on?" I don't know what came over me; I felt a huge sense of love surrounding me and so much support, and the dam burst. I told her everything. OMG, the overwhelming sense of relief I felt when I told her.

I thought my mom was going to have a very difficult time with this information, but she handled it like an absolute pro, an absolute freaking pro! I kept watching for signs of her collapse at the news. Nothing. Yes, she cried. Yes, she was sad. Yes, she was so concerned for me and how I was going to handle it, my surgeries, and my child by myself. But she saw my face. She saw how happy and content I was. I wasn't sad. I wasn't depressed. I wasn't crying. Granted, I had also been given ample time to heal before my mom found out about it, so that was one of the GREATEST benefits of waiting to tell her. Plus, I had already forgiven my ex. THAT was huge! So, I was able to hold a straight face when I told her.

We sat on the couch, and I lay down with my head in her lap. This used to be one of my favorite things to do growing up with my mom. I loved it when she would run her hand through my hair. This time, it brought tears to my eyes, and she was silently sobbing, too. She rubbed my head so lovingly.

Then my massi (my mom's sister), my sweet aunt who lived with my mom, got home from work, so I told her, too, and let the dam break again. It was tears of relief! They were so supportive, sweet, and encouraging. I was so incredibly grateful for their love. It just felt so good to finally get everything out in the open. That was all I ever wanted. And yes, I totally threw my siblings under the bus and blamed them for not allowing me to tell them the truth. LOLOLOLOL. I know, so savage! I'm the black sheep no more, baby! Lol. Sorry, guys! I love you.

Shortly after that, I finally buckled down and went to my pain management doctor, and he scheduled a procedure to shoot me with a steroid epidural in my spine to ease the pain in my sciatic nerve because it was driving me crazy. Even though the marijuana and pain meds were helping me, that sciatic nerve pain just wouldn't go away. I needed to have surgery right after that on my right thumb to have it fused.

Then my cousin called me up and said, "I'm going to Costa Rica in June. Do you want to go with me?" I am very close to this cousin for one particular reason: She also has rheumatoid arthritis, diagnosed at 21. She's also one of the middle-child, black-sheep cousins, lol, so we have that in common, too. Flights were super cheap due to things starting to reopen after COVID, so I could afford a ticket. So, I had my right thumb fused on May 26, 2021, and one month later, I was going to Costa Rica with my cousin with my thumb in a splint. That trip was PHENOMENAL. Keep in mind that I was at peace in my life by that point, and this trip was like my spiritual awakening.

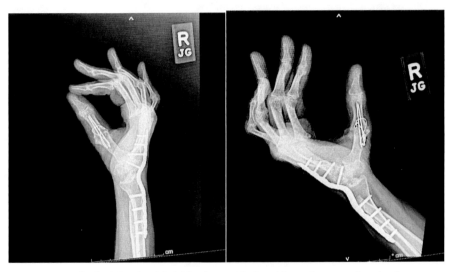

Does this look familiar? Lol. That's my right hand from the cover of my book.
You only saw a part of it. This is the whole deal.

We stayed in a villa called Finca Chilanga on a big hillside in San Mateo, Costa Rica. The views were simply breathtaking. Google it; you'll see. We were in nature, eating farm-grown food. Grounding, exploring nature, enjoying the infinity pool, enjoying peace and quiet. Meditation. Listening to the creatures at night and the rain!!! The rain on the tin roof was oh-so divine! I LOVE THE SOUND OF RAIN! I had already started sleeping to different frequencies and meditations, and anything with rain instantly became my favorite.

This is my favorite pic from my Costa Rica adventure! It was taken by my cousin in the infinity pool at Finca Chilanga, overlooking the gorgeous, peaceful scenery. Absolute bliss.

We went to San Mateo, Orotina, Tertiles, and Jaco. We ate at a five-star restaurant called Villa Caletas on top of a mountain. We drove all the way up and stopped at this little overlook area. Our driver let us jump out of the car and take some pictures. It was a stunning view of the countryside, and we were so far up a mountain! No one could hear us, so my cousin decided to scream at the top of her lungs, "LET THAT SHIT GO!" We were both going through stuff. Lol. And I was like, that was awesome. I'm totally going to do it, too! And I did it! It was so empowering and so wonderful, and I have it on video. It was an amazing release! We drove up the rest of the way and had drinks and appetizers at the gorgeous place overlooking the countryside! The views were INSANE!

The next day, we changed resorts, moving closer to the airport since we were at the end of our trip. We decided to trek out to see a beautiful waterfall. It required a lot of hiking, and I'd had surgery on my foot earlier that year before the thumb fusion. I was like, *Okay, I'll do the best I can.* Sadly, I couldn't go too far. My foot was still healing, but I got to do some of it! And that was more than I ever got to do in San Francisco at the Redwoods! It was a win and felt so good! I didn't get to see the actual waterfall because I didn't make it that far, but my cousin did, and I got to see the pictures she took. It was too far to walk, and the steps leading down to the waterfall were too steep for me. I mean, at the end of the day, my knees and legs can only take me so far. I have to make my joints, real or replacements, last as long as possible. But I was able to do a little bit, and that was all that mattered to me.

After the hike, we went and got massages overlooking the beach on our final night in San Mateo. This is what people always talk about, right? Self-care. I had never done it to this extent. Hell, I had NEVER taken a vacation on my own for pleasure! EVER! Never ever! This was the first time in my life, and I loved it! I vowed that I would do this MORE!

Shortly after I got back from my Costa Rica trip, my ex informed me that he'd lost his job. That included the insurance coverage. This was a hit. It

Me screaming "LET THAT SHIT GO!"

was only June, and I wouldn't qualify for Medicare for another six months. This would be a huge challenge. I had dozens of doctor's appointments and medications that I was on. How was this going to work? I immediately reached out to every single doctor and my pharmacist, who is a very good friend of mine, and came up with a game plan to get the majority of my meds directly through my doctors and pay cash for the ones that were way too expensive.

My pharmacist owns a small local pharmacy, and this woman became my savior over the years. She would deliver medications to my house when I was unable to drive, and she would also go out of her way to find the BEST prices for everything. I am so incredibly blessed to have her in my life!

Also, I was so incredibly fortunate that one of my very good friends moved into my apartment complex. We were both divorced, and our kids lived with us. We immediately became each other's support system. I wholeheartedly believe that everything happens for a reason and there are not a lot of coincidences in life. People come into our lives for a reason, season, or lifetime, and you'll know what category they fall in. This friend is a once-in-a-lifetime type of person. She and I have only increased our bond over the years. She is a lifesaver! She would drop the kids off at school in the morning, and I would do afternoon pickups. It was lifesaving for me because I was still taking painkillers and recovering from surgeries and couldn't drive that early in the morning. However, I still got up to make my daughter's breakfast and school lunch every single morning on the weeks she was with me. It was VERY important to me!

I started a brand-new rheumatoid arthritis medication around this time called Rinvoq, which was an absolute game-changer for me because it worked really well and was easy to use! The Orencia I was on was no longer working. I needed something new, and Rinvoq was a pill, whereas all other RA biologic treatments I had ever been on were self-inject or IV infusions. I loved the idea of not having to inject myself anymore!

I started volunteering for an organization called SoléAna Stables, which is an AMAZING nonprofit whose mission is to empower our military community and people with disabilities and help them discover their unbridled potential through the healing power of horses. The executive director happens to be a friend of mine. When she told me she needed help with their board of directors packet, I told her I would gladly help! I couldn't spend too much time on a computer, given the condition of my hands, but I could do 15 minutes here and 15 minutes there. And it was for a good cause. It was good for my brain to have something to do that only required a small amount of my time, and I was in between surgeries.

We were now approaching the fall of 2021, and my hair was finally the silver fox look I had been going for! After three *loooooooooong* years of looking quite questionable, I'd reached the final point! I'd had two more treatments to remove the old color. My hair was finally exactly what I had envisioned three years before when I'd stopped coloring it. It was my pride and joy. Does that sound sad? It's the little things in life, right? And remember, all I had control over was how I looked. This made me so ridiculously happy!

I wanted to have some fun with my birthday coming up. I was going to be 51, and I had always wanted to do a tasteful boudoir photo shoot. OMG. Let me tell you, it was the best thing that I ever did for myself. Talk about self-care. Talk about women empowerment and everything. Not only did I do a photo session, but I did it in my wedding dress and wedding saris. Gasp! It was so empowering! It was such a beautiful release. For the first time in my life, I was finally starting to love myself – like, genuinely LOVE myself. I had never done that before; I don't even think I really *liked* myself, much less loved myself. This was a foreign feeling to me. If you've ever thought about doing a photo shoot, let me be the one to tell you that it was 100% worth it! The picture on the back cover of this book is one of those pictures. And that's part of my wedding dress. I love this picture because it shows my right shoulder implant and the scars on my shoulder and elbow. Be proud of those scars! They tell a remarkable story.

Shortly after my photo session, I met with my spiritual advisor and decided to have an Akashic Records session. We scheduled it for November 11 at 11:11 a.m. Don't go into an Akashic reading without being prepared. You should be in a good place mentally because it can be super intense. I was in a good place spiritually and mentally. I meditated, prayed, spoke affirmations, and did self-care and healing daily.

In spirituality, when you open your Akashic Records, you can find information from the time your soul was created and about your past lives, present situations, and future possibilities as well. You journey back in time and explore your soul's journey, your past lives, and what lessons you have learned as well as the lessons you have not learned and that keep you in a repetitive pattern of karmic situations. It was a VERY enlightening and eye-opening experience for me! I learned so much from it. The primary takeaway was that I had experienced lifetime after lifetime of trauma. But I always endured. Always. This time was no different. But my purpose was becoming clearer to me. There was a reason I was going through this. I needed to share my story.

In January 2022, Medicare started. I don't like being on disability because I hate the word "disabled." I can't stand it. I also hate the word "handicapped." I did not like to refer to myself using those words. But being on disability allowed me to finally stop life and start listening to my body and healing it. Ever since I stopped working in 2019, I would sleep all day. I slept for most of 2020. It helped me heal. It gave my body the respite I needed to heal. Soooo many decades of damage and destruction had been done to my joints. It wasn't intentional; I just never wanted to stop. I was scared to stop. I wanted to keep going. I wanted to be successful. And I didn't want to be in a wheelchair ever again. But now, I was finally in a position to take care of myself. I would sit in silence and meditate, filled with gratitude for everything that I had and everything that I am. I bought a giant Lovesac from Costco. It's a massive beanbag chair, and I would throw myself on it, put on meditation chakra music, and blissfully zone out. This was my life now – 100% focused on healing.

I was in a zone, my zen, my peace, and really focusing on intentionally praying and meditating. I was forging a deep connection with my entire spiritual team. Through months of healing, I realized that (this is heavy) my spiritual team never abandoned me. It was just as my friend had told me during my reiki session a few years back when she'd said that there was a white light all around me, a presence of so much love. They'd never abandoned me. They'd always been with me. I just hadn't been in a good enough place to see them, feel them, and hear them. Divine timing.

I was listening to kirtan (a traditional Indian chanting practice that involves a group singing in a call-and-response format), hymns, meditations, mantras, and frequencies and praying over my food and water. I never used to do things like that before, but we're made out of matter and water, and if words are so powerful and you have intention behind them, and we pray over our food, why can't we pray over our water? So, I speak healing energy into my water and give gratitude every day, allowing it to heal me. For me, the effect has been unbelievable. Like I said, words are so powerful. Be careful what you say and how you say it. Always speak with intention.

Clearly, I have the foulest mouth. And I'm a goofball. Lol. I wish I could say sorry, but I can't. I cannot apologize because, while it seems to some that I curse a lot, I've also been through a lot. And for me, these words are just words; they simply emphasize my thoughts. They helped me release the pain, the suffering, and ALL THE SHIT. Try walking in my shoes, right? That's Depeche Mode.

I have also become more mindful of who I choose to surround myself with. My energy. My time. My space has become increasingly sacred. My home and my space are my sanctuary. I'm very intentional about who I choose to spend my time with. That's my time. That is my energy, and I don't do energy vampires. I don't have time for anyone who's going to suck the life out of me. I'm not going to do it. I refuse. I insist on spending quality time with the people who actually matter and add value to my life, including family and friends.

I started purging toxic people and things from my life and embracing positive and beautiful souls and beings. We know who's in our inner circle and who is on the outside. Spending quality time with genuine friends and family was imperative to my healing. Today, I actually carve out time to do that. It was never on my radar before. Human connection is imperative to a healthy mental state, but so is solitude. Everything in moderation! As above, so below.

I met a friend in 2021 who, in 2022, brought me some amazing medical-grade marijuana gummies from Denver. I took them and felt fantastic! It was a game-changer! Hell, I thought the stuff that I was getting in the regular smoke shops was working for me and helping with my pain, and it was, it absolutely was, but these gummies? OMG! They were an absolute game-changer.

This prompted me to research medical marijuana again for the state of Texas, and lo and behold! I found out that Texas launched the Compassionate Use Program, but rheumatoid arthritis was not on the list of accepted ailments! *WHAAAAAAAAT?* Why not, Texas? Unbelievable! However, peripheral neuropathy IS on the list of allowable diseases and conditions. So, I made an appointment for a consultation.

For the last ten years, I have maintained a Google doc of my medical history. In it is a list of all of my diagnoses, surgeries, future surgeries, invasive procedures, hospitalizations, ER visits, medical marijuana (MMJ) prescriptions, pharmaceutical prescriptions, "no longer taking" pharmaceutical scripts, supplements, doctors/specialists, and cortisone shots. It's six pages long. There was NO WAY for me to remember all of it. This is what I take with me to every single doctor.

The MMJ doctor was no different. I sent her the document, and during our call, she was floored by my medical history. I told her I was already seeing results with the marijuana that I was consuming and was very excited to try the tinctures that they offered via the two dispensaries in Houston. She told me she'd never had a patient with so much history and said no one qualified more than I did. Lol. Insurance and Medicare don't cover these kinds of treatments, and I was on disability and a very strict budget. I had to make this work. I chose to buy the tinctures and gummies and started my "official" MMJ journey.

I joined the Compassionate Use Program in the state of Texas in July 2022. And that was one of the most important decisions I made in my healing journey! While on this medicinal-quality stuff, I slowly started detoxing from my current pharma medications. From 2021 to 2022, I gradually stopped taking pain medications. Tramadol, Nucynta, Norco, Tizanadene. All stopped. Also Gabapentin, Lyrica, DONE! My sciatic pain was practically gone. One by one, I realized that I didn't need to add them back into my regimen anymore. It was beautiful! I also gradually stopped taking the anti-inflammatories. No more Celebrex. I had been on Celebrex since it came out in 1999!!!! EVERY SINGLE DAY.

I started getting deeper into meditation, learning about sound healing, vibrations, and frequencies and my Indian ancestral ways: breathing techniques, chakras, yoga, cleansing, and Ayurveda. I started sleeping while listening to OM mantras and meditative and healing frequencies. My favorite channel on YouTube is *Meditative Mind*. Different frequencies have the power to heal different chakras and clear blockages in your body. You can heal your entire body from the inside out. I learned the bliss of oneness and being present in the moment, both with myself and others.

I was starting to genuinely LOVE myself. I was becoming increasingly confident! I used to hate my voice on videos, etc. I was VERY critical. Now, I love it! I can listen to my own podcast over and over again. I finally gave myself grace. I apologized to myself for what I've been through. My inner child has been so traumatized my whole life. She was in there, huddled in the corner, crying. I coaxed her out. I apologized profusely for not listening and for letting her down. I begged her to forgive me.

I didn't start true shadow work until 2023 and 2024. It was such a tremendous release of control and allowed me to forgive myself for my past. I used to dwell on the past so much, wondering what if… What if I had been super spiritual while I was in India for six months in such a sacred setting? Would it have made a difference? What if I had married the guy my dad wanted for me in India? What if I had gone on disability earlier? Would it have saved my marriage? So many what-ifs. It had to stop because you can't change the past. The only thing I can control is myself in this present state. That's it. Why torture yourself with what-ifs? How about you focus on what

IS vs. what IF? And if you don't like what IS…then fucking change it! WE ALL HAVE THE ABILITY TO HEAL OURSELVES and CREATE OUR REALITIES. You simply have to believe and release control.

I rejoined a gym. The last time I'd worked out was around 2015. Given the condition of my joints and limitations, I couldn't lift weights or use machines, but I could get in the water and do Aqua Zumba. I went three days a week. It was so beneficial. And the PT I started for my knee replacements in 2020? I was STILL doing it… at least twice a week in addition to the Aqua Zumba. It was all I had. I have chronic fatigue. My body is SO TIRED! This is NOT an exaggeration. It takes me a very long time to get going in the morning. I get up between 8 and 10 a.m., but I stay in bed until 11. I take my supplements on an empty stomach and then have my first meal at noon. I do intermittent fasting and only eat from noon to 7 p.m. daily. That's my window.

I'm also an empath, so I have to be careful around people and their energy. I never used to pay attention to this. I realize now that my energy is incredibly sacred. And I try not to judge because you never know what someone is going through, what their story is. How many people met me over the last ten years and thought I was a horrible person because I was mean and angry? My situation SUCKED! And I took it out on everyone around me, including my ex, my daughter, and our pets! That part is so heartbreaking to me. I was projecting my pain, my suffering, and my anger onto everyone around me and pushing them farther and farther away.

I never used to open my window and give money to the homeless. Why not? Was I judging them? I didn't know their story. So what if they're using that money to buy drugs? I have no idea what they are dealing with. And, more importantly, who the hell am I to judge? I felt ashamed. Now, I make it a point to carry ones and fives whenever I go anywhere, and if I see someone struggling, especially if they are in a wheelchair or are a veteran or a minority, I stop and help. No questions asked. Use the money for anything you want. I feel good blessing others. I don't have a lot myself, but I feel called to share what I have. It's important to me and my healing. I do the same thing with servers and restaurant staff. One of my friends taught me to always tip in cash and write encouraging notes on the receipt. I like doing things that make me feel good and make others feel good. And when I've had exceptional service from someone who truly goes above and beyond, the tip is huge. A little kindness goes a long way.

We humans are so judgy. Why? Stop judging. Look inward! It took me YEARS to look inward. Just imagine how many times I have been judged when I parked in handicapped parking spaces, primarily because I look the way that I look. I've always had amazing hair – black, brown, red, purple, red again, and now gray – and I have piercings – ears, nose, tragus, etc. Even when I was in a wheelchair, people would look at me as if to say, "What are you doing in handicapped parking?" It was so confusing... Do you not see that I'm in a wheelchair? Like, are you blind? Are you stupid? Lol.

There was one moment when I pulled up to Foley's in 1994 and put the handicapped parking tag up. I was not in a wheelchair at this time. It was right after I had the second knee replaced. I got out of my car and was walking into the store when this old woman, a little old white lady, looked at me and said, "Excuse me. That's a handicapped parking spot." And I just looked at her and thought, *Yeah, no shit, dumbass,* but I really wasn't in the mood to fight that day. Usually, I am. LOL! I shook my head and thought, *Not today, Satan. Just not today.* I happened to be wearing my brother's basketball shorts because they were super long and covered up my 12-inch scars. I simply lifted my shorts to where you could see the two red lines going down both of my knees, and her jaw dropped. Just dropped. I didn't have to say anything. I didn't have to do anything. It was the best reaction. She just said, "Oh," and walked away. No apology, nothing. God, it was so annoying. At least I didn't flip her off. I kinda wanted to.

I used to get really angry when people looked at me. Not so much anymore. Today, I kind of wish somebody would approach me and say something. Not to challenge them or say, "It's none of your business." I know it's not! However, if we don't educate each other, what's the point? So, go ahead and ask me. I'll be happy to tell you exactly why I'm in this predicament. You got a few hours to spare? Lol. Buckle up, buttercup. You're about to get schooled! Lol. I feel like my story is so intense that some people don't believe me when I tell them simply *because* of the way that I look. They think there's no way that that's my life story. Again, I don't have control over anything but myself. I have WORKED on myself for the last four years, and it shows. And I look the way that I do because I fucking did the work, man. I did the work, and I'm *still* doing the work. This is not over. It is a lifelong journey of healing.

CHAPTER 12 ½

PHOENIX STILL RISING

MY COSMOS IS MINE
Depeche Mode

I finally got this.
Don't play with me.
Don't mess with me.
Don't question me.
This is MY world!

What's with a Chapter 12 ½? I REALLY wanted 13 chapters in my book and my editors recommended a chapter break at this spot. That would have given me 14 chapters and I really wanted 13. Why 13? 13 is very significant! In Punjabi, 13 is pronounced "thera"... also meaning "yours"... I LOVE THIS!!!! So, here we are. At Chapter 12 ½. Please enjoy...

On February 9, 2022, I had three procedures done on my left hand. My thumb was fused, broken ulna joint fragments were removed, and a lone stitch in my index finger, which had been in my hand since the 2003 MCP implant replacement, was finally removed. My thumb looked weird after the procedure, and I was not happy with the results. It was hyperextending too much, and I asked my surgeon to fix it. I went back on June 8, 2022, to refuse my thumb and realign my tendons. That was my final surgery for a while. It was number 33.

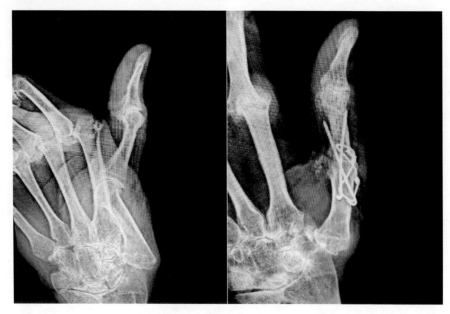

Pre-op and post-op left thumb fusion. Damn! Look how broken my knuckles are and the condition of my left wrist.

I finally had a break for the first time in YEARS! But I was starting to get bored. My podcast partner and I were not consistently recording because we were only doing this for fun. I went through a phase where I missed working, but I also knew that I needed to be on disability for the rest of my life, given the fact that my body and joints are just not the way they used to be. Plus, my right hand isn't what it used to be. I don't have good use of it. Yes, I *look* better now than I ever have in my entire life. Yes, I *feel* better now than I ever have in my entire life. But there's a lot of internal trauma that's not visible, damage to my joints, and I still have chronic fatigue. I am *soooooooo* very tired all the time. My body is very tired. I feel like my mind is more energetic than my body is. It's not a lack of motivation, either. I'm just tired! From the moment I got out of the wheelchair in 1994, I never stopped hustling. NEVER. My brain and my mind are like, "Let's go do this, and let's go do that." But when I get up and start doing things, my body's happy for a bit, but then my "social" meter and "physical" meter drop. Considerably.

Today, I've added lion's mane mushrooms to my diet. It has been helping me with mental acuity, brain fog, and fatigue. I feel more energized while on it. I also started a different MMJ tincture strain from my dispensary, Texas Original, called RSO, which is their version of Rick Simpson Oil. RSO is a very highly regarded MMJ that utilizes the entire marijuana plant. It's darker and thicker in consistency and more of a Sativa versus the Indicas that I was used to. So, I feel slightly more energized during the day now than I used to be.

Back then, I was tired, but I was also very bored and needed something to do with my time. My friend and executive director of SoléAna Stables told me that she had money in her budget to hire a development director and asked me if I was interested. Dang. I knew I couldn't commit to a lot of time, but it would be nice to add a little more income. I wasn't sure I'd be allowed to work while on disability, though, so I called Social Security to check. They told me I wasn't allowed to work more than ten hours a week, which was perfect for me because that's all I was willing to commit to, given my health. And I wasn't allowed to make more than what I was getting with SSDI. That wasn't a problem, either. So, I did it. I became the very part-time development director for SoléAna Stables. And I LOVE IT SO MUCH! It has been an absolute godsend for me! It's beautiful work. It's a wonderful organization that I believe wholeheartedly in!

I'm so grateful to have something to keep my brain busy, and I LOVE horses. They are SO majestic and incredibly healing! I had a special moment when I was doing a session as part of a team builder. I was gently brushing my horse and releasing negative thoughts. All of a sudden, tears welled in my eyes. My horse turned and looked at me as if to say, "It's okay. Let it out." He acknowledged my emotion and encouraged me to let it go. And more tears came out. It was so powerful and cathartic and more divine confirmation that this was the perfect place for me to be!

In late 2022, one of my cousins called me from South Carolina. This cousin is a beast, an absolute beast! I stayed with her in San Francisco several years back when I was still with The Art Institutes, and we did a whole tour of Napa. She used to work for Apple and is incredibly well-educated, doing her undergrad at Duke and with advanced degrees from Harvard and MIT. She's also a middle child like me, and we have always been very close. Mark my words, she is going to change the world someday!

She's deep into Ayurveda, and she invited me to stay with her on Kiawah Island in South Carolina. I booked a flight and stayed with her for ten blissful days. We were in a condo at the Kiawah Island Golf Resort, and let me tell you, I did things I hadn't done in forever, things that I never thought I could physically do again. I used to LOVE riding my bike around the neighborhood when I was young. It was a regular upright bike with two wheels. As an adult, I've had two recumbent bikes with three wheels because I was afraid of falling and injuring myself. I figured that I couldn't ride a regular bike because I'd be screwed if I fell off. With all these surgeries and fusions? Not smart. And I don't exactly have great balance. But the only option in Kiawah Island was an upright bike.

My cousin captured this image of me riding a bike on the beach on Kiawah Island, SC.

I was terrified, but I got on that upright bike and I tried it. And the *main* reason I'd never tried it before was hand brakes. I can't push hand brakes very well because of my hands, but these bikes have a kickstand, and you brake with your pedal, exactly like the bikes I grew up with. OLD SCHOOL. They even had the old-school handlebars and a basket! Lol. I was actually *riding* this bike, and it was the first time I'd been on an upright bike in *decades*. I was riding it on the beach, too, because the beach sand is so compacted on the South Carolina shore that you can ride right up to the water! I think it's one of the rare places in the U.S. where you can do that. It was so badass and peaceful!

I forced myself up at the crack of dawn, and we would ride out to the beach to watch the sunrise every morning. There is nothing more spiritual than greeting the glorious sun while repeating daily affirmations and prayers and meditating. It was magical. We saw stunning sunsets too. We went to Rainbow Row in Charleston and traveled to the sea islands. I never knew South Carolina had sea islands! We learned about the Gullah Geechee. We toured the Penn Center on St. Helena Island. We even visited the cottage where Martin Luther King Jr drafted his "I Have a Dream" speech! We saw so many gorgeous trees with such a violent history of brutal hangings and lynchings. It was so sad. We learned so many things that neither of us ever learned in any history class in school. That day was very overwhelming. While our guides were giving the tour, I hugged so many trees. You could feel the energy, vibration, and history from the awful past. It was quite profound and emotional.

It was very cold during my ten days there, but we loved lying on the beach and soaking up the beautiful sun and magnesium in the sand. I didn't know there was magnesium on the beach! You can soak up magnesium just by lying directly on the sand! My cousin taught me that.

She's big into Ayurveda and adheres to a very natural, very holistic lifestyle. She sat down with me, and we revamped all of my supplements. She has a plethora of knowledge, and I took advantage of her brain. She told me which ones to keep, which ones to remove, which ones provided me zero value in a pill form versus liquid form, and which ones were pure trash. I highly recommend finding someone who knows a lot about supplements to figure out what's going to be the best fit for you! It helped me *so* much. She educated me on eating cleaner, using ghee and olive oil, the value of turmeric, and overall holistic cooking methods. I ate the cleanest, most holistic foods during my ten days with her, and I felt PHENOMENAL!

There's a stunning five-star hotel on Kiawah Island called The Sanctuary, and there's a restaurant in it called Jasmine Porch. Of course, I had to eat there because my name is Jasmine. Duh. I spent $40 on a breakfast buffet there just because my name is Jasmine. Lol. But you can't go someplace and see your namesake and not, you know, appreciate it. The food was just okay, definitely not worth $40; plus, I don't eat that much anyway, so I definitely didn't get my money's worth.

On the beach, we collected gorgeous shells and rescued sand dollars! I had no idea that the fuzzy sand dollars were still alive! We were putting them back in the water. It felt so good! I collected the most unique and biggest shells I had ever seen in my life. I've been to beaches everywhere – I've been to Mexico, Cancun, and Puerto Vallarta, and near Houston, we have Galveston Beach and stuff. And I went to Costa Rica! But I've never seen shells as gorgeous as the ones I saw in South Carolina. I highly recommend making a trip there.

The last thing we did together was talk about a book called *Yoga for Arthritis*. She recommended the book to me. It is really good! Since having my thumbs fused in 2021 and 2022, for the VERY FIRST TIME SINCE MY DIAGNOSIS IN 1984, I can put my hands in prayer pose! I could never do it before due to the deformity in both hands. It was such a magical trip and a beautiful experience. I came back home completely rejuvenated and excited to explore the world of Ayurveda and holistic treatments, food, and more!

I started practicing yoga. There are so many poses that I cannot do because I don't have the range of motion that a normal human being does. I have so many fusions: my thumbs are fused, my right wrist is fused, my right ankle is fused, my big toe is fused, my knees are replaced, my knuckles have been replaced, my shoulder has been replaced. And there are a lot of broken bones and joints that still need to be fixed. I know; it's a lot. I still get overwhelmed sometimes.

A few months after I got back from the Kiawah Island trip, my friend invited me to Denver. This was my first time in Denver since my Art Institute days, but I never got to drive on those trips and always wanted to! It's too flat and boring in Houston. I've always wanted to drive through the mountains and majestic scenery. With my friend, I finally got an opportunity to drive around these beautiful mountains and go back to Red Rocks. We did a trip to the Red Rock Theater when I was with The Art Institutes, and I could barely make that walk. My condition had been so bad that I could barely walk, much less go up and down the stairs inside the theater. It was impossible to truly enjoy the place back then.

But now I was in better shape. I still had to walk slowly, but I was able to do it this time in a way that I had never been able to do before because my knees were so messed up and my joints were in such bad shape. I still couldn't do a whole lot of it, couldn't take *all* the stairs up or anything like that, but with baby steps, I got pretty far! I was inside the theater! And just being able to experience it and stand out there and look down on everything was so empowering and overwhelming.

My friend went ahead of me to take pictures, and I just stood there, taking it all in. They were setting up for a concert that night. Bone Thugs and Harmony, baby! YES!!! It was so awesome! I started tearing up. I never thought the day would come when I'd be able to come back to Denver and do this! It was tiring but well worth it!

Afterward, we drove to Colorado Springs to see a waterfall. I was scared to take the stairs up because they were super steep, so we took the elevator, and I got to enjoy my first waterfall. Remember, I didn't get to see the one in San Mateo, Costa Rica. On our last day, we went to this trippy place called Meow Wolf. OMG! It was *sooooo* cool and super trippy, with very creative and bizarre art. We had a wonderful time. It's been on my bucket list to go back and revisit some of the cities and states that I traveled to back in my Art

Me in Colorado Springs 2023.

Institute days, and Denver was on that list! It was so nice to be able to cross that one off. And yes, I explored some really good MMJ while I was there!

My life is so very different now because I have faith and hope, two things I had somehow lost somewhere along my journey, and I am so grateful to have them back. My beautiful spiritual team, I know they never abandoned me. And faith in my higher power, faith in source, faith in God, faith in infinite spirit, faith in Waheguru, faith in all of the above, has been such an awakening for me, just having that conscious awareness, that self-awareness, having empathy, having compassion.

As an empath, I feel other people's energy, so it's really important for me to guard my energy and make sure that I'm okay. I have a tendency to take on other people's pain and suffering because I know I can handle it. I've been through so much in my life that I feel like, "Just give me more. It's okay. I can handle it. I can take it." But I have to stop doing that now. I cannot do that anymore. I need to be more protective. I've been digging into shadow work and doing shadow work journaling. I've been digging into my past, digging into trauma, and just forgiving myself and really working with my inner child and trying to heal that trauma, valuing my personal time and space.

Being on disability, my income dropped drastically. I was receiving SSDI, dependent disability (for my daughter), and also child support. It would only last until she turned 18. I had several conversations with my daughter about how there might come a time when I could no longer afford a two-bedroom apartment and that, most likely, once she turned 18, and I lost the dependent disability and child support, I'd have to downsize, and she would have to move in with her dad. Somehow, I thought I'd have time, but then my ex was moving in the summer of 2023, and he decided to get a place with a room for our child. So, in August of 2023, my daughter moved out.

She had been living with me primarily since August 2020. And this child is my absolute pride and joy. I knew her moving out would be a very pivotal moment and *really* test my depression levels. I was scared for the first time since February 2020. I was doing so well health-wise and didn't want to have a setback. She is my everything. My life. My reason. And she moved out. I cried in the weeks leading up to it, helping her pack. We had several tender moments, but we both knew this was for the best. And maybe there would come a time when she could come back home to me when my circumstances changed. Who knows! I cried after she left.

But then the strangest thing happened. I wasn't depressed. I wasn't sad. How? I tried to force myself to cry, but I couldn't. Was I a bad mom? Did this make me a bad mom? I was so grateful that I didn't take a dive into a deep, dark place. Instead, I looked inward and worked on myself. And I KNEW she was happy–that definitely helped! I did more shadow work and continued to make myself stronger, realizing that my personal space is critical to me, valuing my alone time, loving myself, and giving myself attention. Self-care. It was AMAZING! I wasn't depressed. And she didn't move that far away, either. She was in the same complex as me, in the next building in fact! Lol. That made it better, too.

The amount of work I have done on myself since living alone has been incredible! I value my peace and solitude so much. I've thought about being in another relationship, but it's hard when you have so much medical history. It's overwhelming. It'll take a very special person to be able to handle all of me. All of this. And I quite enjoy myself and my company.

I also know I still have more surgeries that need to happen. I still need to have my left shoulder replaced. I need to have the exact same surgery that I had on my right shoulder. I need to have my knuckles re-replaced. My middle finger on the right hand is broken. It needs to be fused. The toes on my left foot have started to lift up again and dislocate. At some point, I'll need to have them straightened again. I've had that same surgery SO MANY times on both feet. Lol. It's so annoying.

All that is to say that I count my blessings every single day! Why? I'm in remission from peripheral neuropathy. I still have numbness in my hands and my feet, but I don't have the massive nerve pain or the brutal sciatic nerve pain.

I'm in remission from chronic pain. It has been steadily decreasing since 2020.

I'm in remission from ulcerative colitis, and my colon is squeaky clean. You should have seen the before-and-after pictures.

I no longer have high blood pressure, an elevated heart rate, liver issues, or chronic dry eye disease.

On August 9, 2023, I was sitting on the couch with my daughter when I got a phone call from my rheumatologist's office to give me my LabCorp Vectra test results.

The Vectra test:

The Vectra Report gives a molecular assessment of RA disease. Vectra demonstrates its unsurpassed ability to predict radiographic progression as a personalized inflammatory measure for patients with RA. Vectra, used with provider and patient assessments, helps guide better patient outcomes.

Rheumatoid arthritis (RA) is a systemic disease that can be difficult to manage. Providers can add an objective measure to an assessment with Vectra.

Vectra provides a personalized score by measuring 12 biomarkers and incorporating information on age, gender, and adiposity to measure your patients' RA inflammation and predict their risk of radiographic progression.

Year after year, this Vectra test of mine would fluctuate from the 40s to the 50s. This time, the nurse said, "Your Vectra level is 14."

"Wait, what?" I said. "Did you say 40-something?"

"No, I said 14, one-four!"

"No way!" I exclaimed, and I immediately started crying like a baby. What does that mean? Does that mean I'm in remission?"

"Yeah," she replied.

I was like, "Oh, my God, are you serious?" Y'all!!!!! It'd been 40 years since the moment of diagnosis in 1984, and I'd *never* been in remission. I'd gone into remission very briefly during the pregnancy, but that was a false sense of remission due to the pregnancy. Once the pregnancy was over, it hit me once again like a Mack truck.

For the *first time in 40 years*, I was in true remission. I FINALLY heard those words!!! And it was fucking unbelievable. This is what it feels like to manifest your reality. This was a *HUUUUUUGE* leveling up for my soul and further solidified my purpose. NOW it was time to finally share my story. NOW I had the ending that I had been waiting for 40 FUCKING YEARS! This was the one thing I never thought would be possible for me. And it just happened! So, if *this* can happen, that means *anything* is possible.

I started digging more into manifestation and visualization, gratitude journaling, recording myself and my thoughts, and just really keeping track of who I am as a human being and my purpose. What can I do to help humanity and contribute in a positive way? There has to be a reason why I went through what I did. Surely, it can't have been for nothing. Hell, I finally had the ending to my book. But I had no clue where to start.

People have been telling me my whole life, "You should write a book. You should tell your story," but I'd never thought anyone would want to read it, honestly. I lived it, and to me, it wasn't that big of a deal. I feel as though I did what anyone would have done in my shoes. Apparently, that's not the case. At least, that's not what people tell me after they hear my story. But I couldn't really "write" my story physically. It was too much to type, and I didn't know where to start. I had dozens of recordings and had used voice-to-text in Google Docs to create a manuscript, but I was too critical, and the voice-to-text looked like mumbo jumbo to me. The manuscript was roughly 35 pages long.

I still didn't know how to do this. All I knew was that it was finally time for me to share it.

Then, a window opened. My friend Anglea Burgess wrote a book called *Are You on the Right Bus?:Navigating Change on the Road to Success*, which was published. She referred me to the publishing company and shared a little about my story with them. The CEO of the publishing company connected with me on LinkedIn. I recognized her name from my friend's book launch, reached out to her immediately, and told her that I'd been thinking about writing my book for YEARS but couldn't physically write. We scheduled a chat, and I learned that their process was to record the author *speaking* their story, which would ultimately produce a manuscript. And here we are. I am so incredibly blessed to be able to share my healing journey with you!

CHAPTER 13

I FEEL LOVED

I FEEL LOVED

Depeche Mode

For the first time in my life,
I felt true love.
ALL around me.
Not just from others.
Not just from music, but from ME!
For the very first time in my ENTIRE life,
I loved MYSELF!
Unconditionally.

Out of the deepest respect for its impact on my life, I must devote my final chapter to music. After all, it is the consistent theme in my story and truly one of the most important pieces of my life and healing journey.

Simply put, music made me feel loved.

It embraced me, took care of me, transported me to places I had never been, and soothed me.

And it *healed me to my core.*

There's a song by Depeche Mode called "Higher Love" that has always impacted me so much throughout my life! The concert where they opened the show with this song was the only one I went to while in a wheelchair.

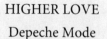

HIGHER LOVE
Depeche Mode

I did it!
I FUCKING did it!
I rose above it all.
A higher love was there all along.
I was lifted by a higher power.
By a higher love.

Jasmine was back. Jasmine was healed. A higher love embraced me.

And here's another reason I wanted 13 chapters in my book. I was a member of Depeche Mode's Fan Club, and they used to send me the official fan club magazine titled *Bong*. The last edition I received was issue #13, and it was signed by the band!

And here's a "small" part of my Depeche Mode Collection minus all apparel:

Music has been in my soul from the get-go. I don't think I would be where I am today without music. I always said that I missed my calling to be a DJ. I used to record my own mix tapes and splice the music on my boombox, and a lot of the mixes were pretty damn seamless! I still have the cassettes with the mixes I made. The energy when you first hear a song, the happiness, the places that you're transported to are unbelievable. Even if the memory is a bad or sad one, music transports you back to a time you can't even fathom, like surviving a bad car accident or going to your 20th surgery. Sometimes, I get so overwhelmed when I share my story. Did I really go through all of that? Like, it's just so much!

Whenever I attend a party, a function, or anything, I always ask, "Where's the music?" Because if there's no music, I'm not staying, lol. I don't like complete silence unless I'm meditating. Music soothes me so much. I have music on all day while I'm working, cleaning, cooking, driving, sleeping, ALL THE TIME! If I'm concentrating on something, I'll put on meditative music in the background without any lyrics, something very calm and relaxing. But if I don't really need to focus that much, I'm just having a good time, or I need to be motivated, I'll put on something more "dancy," like EDM, 80s or 90s dance or hip hop, or reggaeton.

I also take periodic dance breaks throughout the day. I only work two hours a day, and I try to spread my time out so I'm not sitting down in one position for too long. It takes a toll on my body, especially with my sciatic nerve issue. That's in remission, and I'm determined to keep it that way! So, I make sure that I move around a lot, and I get up and have my own little five-minute dance party. I used to dance with glow sticks at club Prague and raves. It kept my arms in shape! My knees were in such bad shape before I had them re-replaced. It's a miracle I'm even able to dance again!

Funny story: When I was working with The Art Institutes as a rep, I always had music playing while students were entering the classroom for my presentations. I also used to play cool visualizations on the screen. Remember those? The cool music players we would use to play music and change the skin and visuals to your liking? I used to play "The Word" by Dope Smugglaz (remixed by Paul Oakenfold). It was so badass! Not only did I have music playing, but I had to have the BEST speakers. I invested big time! The company only reimbursed us for cheap speakers, and I don't do cheap speakers. I do not compromise on my music! Lol. So, I found these badass JBL speakers. There were two speakers with a subwoofer, part of JBL's Creature series. They were a beautiful silver color and looked kind of like Darth Vader's helmet. They were *sooooo* cool! The students loved them, and I got to enjoy music all day long. It added that extra element to my presentation that none of the other reps had. Later, JBL released the speakers in a stunning royal red! They were majestic!!! All of the high school students thought I was the coolest presenter they'd ever seen because of the speakers and the music I played. I also wore Dr. Martens… that's always cool, too! Sadly, I can't wear Dr. Martens anymore because they are too heavy for my feet.

Once I got on the presentation design team for AI, I took that up a notch because I was in charge of picking portfolio pieces. I always chose pieces that had fantastic music in the background so the presentation would be super fun for me and my audience. I loved doing that kind of stuff. I took so much pride in it!

Speakers have ALWAYS been critical for me! I had boomboxes with the best bass. I had that badass Technics system at my parents' house, which had so much bass. I had my brother's Nissan Stanza pimped out with two 12-inch kickers in the trunk and an amp with a switch under my seat. I also got badass wheels and rims for the car and got the windows tinted to the darkest legal color I could get. The car looked and sounded AMAZING! My sound system was VERY important to me! The only downside was that the speakers and box took up the entire trunk. Lol. Then, when I moved out and on my own, I bought my very first car: a silver Hyundai Tiburon with a pretty good sound system. It was a sports car! True story: I actually LOVE cars! Especially when I can zip around in them, and it's best when the sound system is up to my standards! I even took that car to get silver/mirrored tint on the windows to match the whole silver theme. It looked pretty cool!

With The Art Institutes, we always had company cars. I inherited a white Chevy Impala with a baby blue interior because that was the car my predecessor chose prior to quitting her position. I often thought she did it on purpose because it was SOOOO ugly. That color combo. Gross. Not my taste. I like BLACK… everything. Lol. I was pissed, but whatever. I got in and turned on the radio. Oh, MYLANTA!!!!! What kind of sorcery was this? The speakers were BUMPING! I was dumbstruck. How the hell could a car THIS ugly have such an amazing sound system? I realized there was an amp in the car, too! WHAT? I was in heaven! It was so great, in fact, that my next car was also an Impala, but this time, I got to choose my colors (black with gray interior). Then I had to downsize due to my health and settled for a Chrysler Sebring.

Finally, we stopped doing the company cars, and I could get my own vehicle and just have an amazing sound system. I was able to get into an Acura TSX with metal racing pedals and red details inside. And the system was AMAZING! That's how I choose my cars. To this day, I choose my car based on the sound system. I don't care about the make, model, or anything. Well, I DO care, but it's not how I base my decision. I want a badass sound system in my car. That is critical for me and my soul. My current Audi Q3 is a base model. No cool display with navigation, etc. NADA. But I have a KILLER sound system! And that's enough!

I've come such a long way! When I was younger, I used to listen to any radio I could find. We used to have those tiny clock radios that were battery-operated; I would sneak them into the bathroom just to listen to music. My mom didn't like me listening to music as much as I wanted to listen to music. If it had been up to me, I would have listened to music 24/7 when I was a kid, but I wasn't allowed to do that. So, I would sneak radios at home and borrow Walkmans from my friends so I could listen to the radio or their cassettes on the bus and in school.

Growing up, at home, we primarily listened to kirtan and prayers. I had my favorite Ragis (musicians who sing the ragas/melodies), and I enjoyed listening to them. And I haven't even mentioned all of the times that I went to Gurdwara and fell into a blissful trance from the hymns that were being sung or the Shaan that they would play at the start of the daily services. Those tunes were my favorites!! A Shaan is basically an instrumental piece traditionally played in the Raag at the beginning of kirtan. It is a simple tune that starts slow and progressively speeds up. It is so entrancing! There was a time in my life when I could actually play some of them on the harmonium until my hands got too bad. I loved listening to them, and I loved playing them! Kirtan, in general, is so incredibly meditative, relaxing, and healing.

A harmonium, also called a "reed organ" or "pump organ," is a keyboard instrument that is a lot like an organ. Sound is made by blowing air through reeds, which are tuned to different pitches to make musical notes. My sister and I learned classical music and ragas from a Ragi at our Gurdwara, and we also taught ourselves how to read and write our native language, Punjabi. We already spoke it at home but never quite grasped the alphabet. I was definitely a slower learner than my sister, but I got it, too!

The harmonium is similar to a keyboard in that it has keys. One of my very good high school friends was leaving for college while I was in a wheelchair in 1991, and she brought over her electric keyboard for me to play. I composed my own tunes and also made mash-ups with some of my favorite tunes, like Salt & Pepa's "Push It," Depeche Mode's "Lie to Me," and so many other songs. (Sidebar: I could play Depeche Mode's "Pimpf" from their album *Music for the Masses* in its entirety!) I was self-taught! I could listen to a song and play it perfectly on the keyboard! I also added "Axel F" from the *Beverly Hills Cop* movie soundtrack. I LOVED that song so much!

There were so many songs that I mashed up and played on the keyboard and even added percussions and other instruments in the background. Not to toot my own horn, but it was *so good* that my parents would ask me to play it whenever we had company over! And they would also ask me to show everyone my artwork. This goes to show that while they didn't want me to major in art, music, or anything creative, they were proud of me and my skills and liked showing me off! It's the little things in life that truly matter, right?

Now, let's talk about Michael Jackson. His music was brilliant. "Billie Jean" is my go-to. Like, if I hear "Billie Jean" in public and you know me, you're automatically going to think, "Oh, shit, she's going to start dancing, and it's about to go down." Everyone who knows me well knows this about me. I can sing the entire song. I can't dance like Michael, but I like to think that I can. Lol. One time at a piano bar, we were celebrating a friend's birthday, and the band started playing "Billie Jean." Yeah, I was up on stage, dancing and singing. Another time, we were at TGI Fridays, and as we stood up to leave, the riff for "Beat It" started. Dun, dun. Dun, dun... Immediately, my child looked at me and said, "Oh, no, Mommy, are you going to start dancing?"

I was like, "Yeah, baby, you know, it's true. I'm going to start dancing." There was a family next to us who overheard this exchange and started cracking up. Lol. It was so funny. Everybody who knows me knows that any song by MJ is my weakness. I'm *gonna have to* dance.

I loved dancing and showing off my Michael Jackson moves to my family, just like I used to disco dance back in the 70s. I have listened to every genre throughout my life, but it all started with disco. Diana Ross, Donna Summer, Stevie Wonder... The show *Solid Gold*! OMG. I wanted to be a *Solid Gold* dancer so badly. The women were gorgeous and wore stunning gold leotards with heels, and I wanted to dance like them! I also used to watch *Soul Train*. I wanted to dance on that show and be a part of it all. I wanted to experience it myself. I loved the BeeGees and *Saturday Night Fever*. WOW! That was the most amazing record at that time, 1977, baby! *Every single song* on that record was fire! I Freaking loved it.

Every year on New Year's Eve, PBS would broadcast live from the Championship Ballroom Dancing Competition, and I was GLUED to the TV. It lasted several years, and I never missed it! I would stay up until midnight to find out the winners! I loved dancing and watching dance competitions. It never stopped. It simply evolved into shows like *So You Think You Can Dance*, *World of Dance*, and even *The Ellen DeGeneres Show*! I never missed an episode of any of these shows! I loved watching Ellen so much. She made me so happy from 2003 up until COVID, when things fell apart. I always wanted to be a guest on her show and dance with her and tWitch. It's so sad about tWitch. I was absolutely devastated when I found out he had passed. He was my favorite dancer, both on *So You Think You Can Dance* and on *Ellen*. I would block out time to watch *Ellen* every single day. I even got my daughter into *SYTYCD* and took her to see the live shows twice when they toured, and we got to see tWitch!

Do you remember in the 90s when a unique band emerged that combined chanting monks with chill, relaxing, seductive music? That was Enigma, and they blew me away! They were the first band that made me

WANT TO explore meditation, visualization, and relaxation. The music was *sooooooo* good and *soooooo* different than anything else at the time. Then I got into more relaxing music like Massive Attack, Tricky and Delirium. And what can I say about the neo-soul genre? So good! Maxwell, India Arie, Sade, Mazzy Star. As for alternative music, of course, my favorite is Depeche Mode, followed by Pet Shop Boys, New Order, The Cure, Nine Inch Nails, Meat Beat Manifesto, KMFDM, Front 242, and so many more! I have been incredibly blessed to have seen so many of these performers live because "music is my life" (shoutout to Snap!). My entire life revolves around music!

And how can I forget rap and R&B? You CANNOT have two 12s in your trunk and not drive around "Bumpin' My Music" (shoutout to Ray Cash and Scarface). I love all of the H-Town folks, UGK, Slim Thug, Scarface, "Paul Wall, baby, whatchu know about me," and "Mike Jones, Mike Jones, the one and only, you can't clone me, got a lotta haters and a lotta homies, some friends and some phony." YES! For those of you who understood those references, they're from one of my favorite rap songs, "Still Tippin'." I actually considered titling this book "Still Tippin'." It fits so well! I'm still here, and I'm still tippin'! LOL!

I love Ice Cube, Dre, Snoop, NWA, Bone Thugs & Harmony, and Cypress Hill, my girls Missy Elliott, Aaliyah, Salt-N-Pepa, SWV, and TLC, and my own Punjabi heritage Bhangra music and other Indian music!!! Punjabi MC, Dalgit Dosanjh, Bally Sagoo, and Kahani are a few, along with my good friend DJ Impact from DBI Dhol Beat International. DJ Impact went to high school with my brother before he became a DJ, and we used to talk about music all the time! This was during my four years in a wheelchair. I was so grateful to have someone to talk with who shared my passion for music and creating mashups and remixes!

Later, when I went back to college after the first knee replacements, I joined the Indian Student Association, where my cousin was the president, and DJ Impact created a mix CD for us to use during the Indian/Punjabi Fashion Show at our year-end gala. It was so badass! It was 20 minutes long and called *Existential Sphinx*, and it featured so many popular Indian songs, mostly Punbaji Bhangra from the 90s. I still listen to it today, and it has become one of my daughter's favorite mixes to listen to as well.

My true passion for music is with anything I can dance to. ANY dance music. Anything with a beat that gets you off of your ass and on the floor! It started with Lipps Inc.'s "Funkytown" and evolved into Michael Jackson, Stevie B, Snap!, techno, drum and bass, BPM, house, trance, The Prodigy, Chemical Brothers, Polygon Windows, Aphex Twin, Above & Beyond, Kaskade, Deadmau5, Eli & Fur, and my current obsession, REZZ! She's BRILLIANT!!! My very first full-blown rave with an actual famous EDM DJ was Paul Oakenfold. It was pure magic! Oh, my God, to this day, I cannot wait to get to the Ultra Music Festival in Miami, EDC in Las Vegas, Tomorrowland, Electric Daisy Carnival, or any festival where they have EDM artists and badass visualizations.

I used to make mix CDs of my favorite dance songs and dance while pregnant and also with my baby in the Baby Bjorn after I gave birth! My child's favorite DJ was Deadmau5! Fast forward 16 years and I took my child to her first rave the day after Thanksgiving Day in 2022. We saw Deadmau5. It was so cool! My child saw a side of me that she had NEVER seen before. She'd only heard me tell her stories of how her mom used to be so cool! Lol. Yes, I would get the eye roll for that. "Yeah, sure, Mom, you were SO cool!" Ha! I used to dance with glowsticks back in my clubbing and raving days, but I can't hold the glowsticks now due to the condition of my hands. For this show, I wore LED gloves. We were directly in front of the stage, and my kid got to see mom "pop off," as the kids say, or "she ate and left no crumbs." Lol. She was shocked! And it was so great to watch her watching me in my element! It was such a beautiful moment for us, definitely a core memory for me right next to giving birth to her – my little miracle and pride and joy. I don't think she knows just how special that night was for me. We had come SO FAR together! It was so special and overwhelming! We have also seen Lady Gaga twice together and I saw Gaga with a good friend two times prior to my child being old enough to go! PAWS UP!!! And Lady Gaga is such an inspiration as well dealing with autoimmune issues herself. What a warrior!

The greatest benefit of dancing has always been that it allows me to stay in shape! This is why I get up and dance during the day to break the monotony. It's helpful to my joints, and it helps me stay in shape! I love it so much.

I went through an unbelievable journey with my health, and music allowed me the escape that I needed to shelter myself from the storm. I played the keyboard, composed mixes and mashups, and then recorded live club broadcasts from Detour. I created these cassettes, and I mixed them on my own. I spliced them with other songs and audio samples. I was basically DJing using a boombox with two cassette decks. That was the only equipment that I had back then. Pretty impressive. What I was able to do with such limited resources was amazing!

When I was finally able to go to Club Spy and Prague after college, I had VIP cards and was reunited with some of the DJs I used to speak with over the phone while in a wheelchair. It was so cool! I would go there from 10 p.m. to 2 a.m., anywhere from two to three times a week, every week, for almost a year. My unofficial "job" was to get the dance floor going. I would go out onto the dance floor and start dancing, and then everybody else would surround me. It was so empowering for me! It was my happy place. It was the way that I worked out, exerted my energy, and just danced. All I wanted to do was get lost in the music and dance.

Now, when it's time to wind down or focus on my goals and my purpose, I turn to meditative frequencies. *Meditative Mind* is one of my favorite YouTube channels. I love listening to "Chakra Cleansings" and "Om Chanting." They give me peace. My current obsession is handpan music! So beautiful and relaxing!

Music quite literally saved me from a deep, dark depression. When I was younger, I would fall asleep listening to music, dreaming of dancing again someday, one day. I visualized having my life back. I didn't know when it would happen, but I knew it would. I had faith, and faith is so important. It doesn't matter what that faith is. The only thing that matters is that you *have* faith.

So, dear music, thank you for saving me.

Thank you for transporting me to all of those good times and memories. You have always been my escape, my sanctuary. You set me free. You allow me to be unapologetically crazy, sarcastic, funny, and my authentic self. This is who I am. There's a song by one of my favorite DJs, Gareth Emery, called "Sanctuary" that encompasses exactly what music provides for me.

SANCTUARY

Gareth Emery

This is one of my absolute favorite dance songs!
This is what music did for me.
It saved me from my trauma.
When I had nowhere to go, nowhere left to run,
Music saved my soul.
It provided me with a healing sanctuary for my soul.

I choose to live as the person I am now, in this moment, today. Not the person that I once was. I choose to be happy. Every. Single. Day. I'm nowhere near done healing because there's no such thing, right? You can never be *done* healing. It's a never-ending journey. I believe it's a soul journey. We are constantly healing. We are constantly learning, evolving, leveling up, and ascending into higher beings.

The song "Home" by Depeche Mode always brings tears to my eyes because it's a beautiful song, and the message is so loving. This message is a very heartfelt one dedicated to my entire spiritual team to thank them for never leaving my side, for never abandoning me:

HOME

Depeche Mode

As many times as I have seen Depeche Mode in concert,
I had never seen them perform this song until 2023.
I was healed.
I was in remission from everything.
I went to the show with my baby girl.
And I cried my eyes out during this song.
Thank you music.
Thank you Depeche Mode.
Thank you for bringing me here, in this moment, with my child.
I finally belong.
Here.
I'm HOME.

This could be you, too. Anyone can do this. I'm living proof.

My final thought: You cannot live your life in a constant state of fear. That's what I did, and it almost buried me. I was terrified of being wheelchair-bound or having to apply for disability again. Therefore, I kept going until my body shut down. I was terrified of being alone, so I tried my best to hold onto a marriage that I simply knew was falling apart. And as much as I wanted to end it all and wanted to be gone, I was terrified of death. Once those fears dissipated, one by one, I started to heal. I started to mend the damage that had been done. I started to blossom. I started to rise like a motherfucking phoenix and scream to the whole world that the cure for everything is to LET THAT SHIT GO because letting things go and releasing the past also releases the *fear* of the unknown. And like Boris Brejcha says in his song "Fear," everything you could ever want is on the *"OTHER SIDE"* of fear!

So, what are you waiting for? GO GET IT!

CONCLUSION

As I sit here and reflect on my past, it's daunting to think that ALL of those things happened to me, and I'm only 53. There's so much that I didn't say in this book. Dealing with autoimmune diseases for 40 years, wheelchair-bound for four years, 36 surgeries (so far) – it's so much. But the big question is, would I do it all over again if it meant being where I am and who I am today? ABSOFUCKINGLUTELY! This peace, this zen, it feels *SOOOOOOOOOO* good! This journey has been *insane*, with so many twists and turns, and I survived it all.

Me, in deep reflection... lol

I know it's a lot, right? Trust me, I cried my eyes out throughout this entire process. It was such a therapeutic purge for me. And now I can move on. I've let it all go. I've forgiven.

Remember the tough boss that I had right before my UC diagnosis, who was so critical of everything that I did? She reached out to me on LinkedIn and apologized. I was floored. The apology came six years after it happened. It took me a few days for me to process her message and the apology, and when I finally responded, it was with heartfelt forgiveness.

We humans cannot survive without purging, forgiving, letting go, and moving on. We need to FREE our minds and our souls for what's coming next rather than focusing so much on the past and what has already happened because we can't change it. It will never change. So, who cares? LET THAT SHIT GO!

Be in the present; live in the present. You cannot change the past, and you cannot predict the future, but you can damn sure do everything in your power to be happy and at peace *in this moment.*

Today, I'm still on disability and probably will be for the rest of my life. And that's ok. I've made peace with that. I've made self-care my primary focus, and I'm *still* healing. I still deal with chronic fatigue and serious brain fog, but lion's mane mushroom powder has been helping. I also work out three days a week doing Aqua Zumba and Pilates (both of them are low impact on your joints). And I have a massage membership so I can get one every month. I never did these things for myself before. Not consistently, anyway, but they are so critical for my body to stay active and healthy.

Thank you for allowing me to share my story and my healing journey with you! I'm so grateful for you. It's been a VERY long road, but I know there's more to life, and I welcome it with open arms!

If you would like to get in touch with me, you may do so via my Linktree. And keep an eye out for a website in the near future.

Finally, thank YOU, my sweet reader, for taking this trip with me, all around my world and back! And thank YOU for allowing me to show you the "World in My Eyes"!

THANK YOU FOR READING MY BOOK!

Just to say thanks for buying and reading my book,
I want to share my special playlist.

Scan the QR Code:

I appreciate your interest in my book and value your feedback as it helps me improve future versions of this book. I would appreciate it if you could leave your invaluable review on Amazon.com with your feedback. Thank you!

Made in United States
North Haven, CT
27 November 2024

61033657R00138